KU-546-616

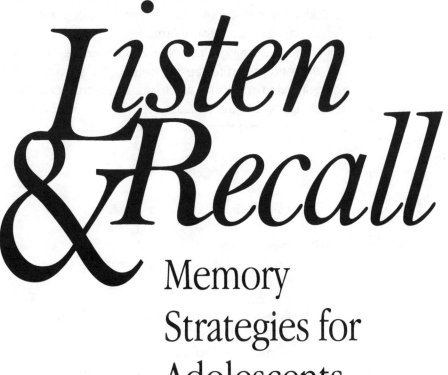

Listen &Recall

Memory Strategies for Adolescents and Adults

by Carrie van der Laan, M.A.

Thinking Publications
Eau Claire, Wisconsin

© 1997 by Thinking Publications®
A Division of McKinley Companies, Inc.

Thinking Publications grants limited rights to individual professionals to reproduce and distribute pages that indicate duplication is permissible. Pages can be used for instruction only and must include Thinking Publications' copyright notice. All rights are reserved for the pages without the permission-to-reprint notice. No part of these pages may be reproduced in any form, electronic or mechanical, including photocopy, recording, or any information storage and retrieval system without permission in writing from the publisher.

08   07   06   05   04   10   9   8   7   6   5

Cataloging-in-Publication Data

Laan, Carrie van der.
   Listen and recall : memory strategies for adolescents and adults / by Carrie van der Laan.
      p.   cm.
   Includes bibliographic references.
   ISBN 1-888222-00-X (pbk.)
      1. Listening—Problems, exercises, etc.   2. Memory—Problems, exercises, etc.   3. Mnemonics.   I. Title.
   BF323.L5L22   1997
   153.1'4—dc21   97-198
                                                        CIP

Cover Design: Mindy Merryfield
Illustrations: Robert T. Baker
Printed in the United States of America

**THINKING
PUBLICATIONS®**
A Division of McKinley Companies, Inc.

424 Galloway Street • Eau Claire, WI 54703
715.832.2488 • Fax 715.832.9082
Email: custserv@ThinkingPublications.com

COMMUNICATION SOLUTIONS THAT CHANGE LIVES®

Table of Contents

PAGE

Preface v

Introduction 1

   Overview of *Listen and Recall* .1

   Assumptions Underlying *Listen and Recall* 4

   Identifying Individuals with Inefficient Memory Strategies 5

   Description of *Listen and Recall* Sections 12

   Using *Listen and Recall* 13

   Generalization 21

Section I: Retention and Recall of Spoken
Unrelated Words 23

   Rationale 23

   Presentation 25

   Word Lists 33

   Word List One 35

   Word List Two 36

   Word List Three 37

   Summary 38

Section II: Retention and Recall of Spoken Facts 41

   Rationale 41

   Materials 41

   Presentation 42

   Monitoring Progress 47

   Generalization 49

Section III: Retention and Recall of Information
in Spoken Articles 53

   Rationale 53

   Materials 54

   Presentation 56

   Monitoring Progress 59

   Section III Lessons 62

Section IV: Retention and Recall of Oral Directions 103

   Rationale 103

   Materials 103

   Presentation 104

   Monitoring Progress 104

Section IV Lessons 105

Appendices 143

Appendix A: Checklist of Informal Indicators
of Memory—Version 1 145
Appendix B: Checklist of Informal Indicators
of Memory—Version 2 146
Appendix C: Progress Sheet 147
Appendix D: Steps to Success .148
Appendix E: Illustrated Card Sets 149
Appendix F: Stimulus Cards 164
Appendix G: Maps 189
Appendix H: Counting Facts 191

References 195

Preface

The needs and efforts of adolescents in Norwood, MA, inspired the creation of these materials to teach listening and memory skills. When I first began working with high school students, testing revealed that many had auditory memory deficits, but there were few materials to address this problem and none that were practical and applicable to real-life situations. I needed materials that went beyond word and sentence repetition—ones that would make a significant difference in the way individuals listened. Through research, experimentation, and feedback, these materials evolved. The first edition of *Listen and Recall* was titled *ALP: Active Listening Program.* I have now used the memory strategies from *ALP* successfully with students in grades 6 through 12 for over a decade. It has been a pleasure to see students improve and gain confidence in their listening and memory skills. It also is rewarding to observe them applying these listening strategies in their daily lives.

Listen and Recall also teaches memory strategies. It is a structured program that allows adolescents (age 11 and older) or adults to experiment with and choose memory strategies that will significantly improve their attention to and recall of oral information. The process begins with activities to recall words and steadily progresses to recalling lengthy passages and oral directions. Generalization suggestions encourage the use of memory strategies in real-life situations. The materials can be used with individuals or with groups. Individual success is ensured because the materials are highly adaptable in pacing and in difficulty. This second edition includes additional memory strategies and ideas to encourage use of materials in daily life situations.

Much of the initial support and encouragement for the development of *Listen and Recall* came from Elisabeth Wiig, who gave generously of her time, expertise, enthusiasm, and professionalism. Her dedication to the field of speech-language pathology and to individuals with communication disorders is remarkable and is much appreciated.

Many friends have given personal encouragement, insights, and perceptions. I specifically want to thank Alice Axelrod, Mary Bell, Bill Joplin, Judy Friedman, Carol Siemering, Aurelie Jones Goodwin, and George Corbett.

Nancy McKinley's enthusiasm and support helped the first edition to solidify. Her encouragement during the second edition has led to an improved and more comprehensive resource. She approached all work with a cheerful and positive manner. Sue Schultz, editor, has provided expertise and sound practical suggestions based on her experience working with high school students. She contributed helpful suggestions; her insight has contributed to making this resource more practical and easier to use. And I appreciate Linda Schreiber's patient approach to detail and organization.

Introduction

Overview of *Listen and Recall*

The retention or memory of information heard is vital in school as well as outside of school. In fact, memory plays a central role in nearly every human activity (Cowan, 1996). Through the school years, different levels of listening and retention are expected. When students advance to the upper elementary grades, junior high, and high school, they are required to listen to and remember progressively more information. The information becomes more complex, and students are expected to work more independently. Often in middle school or junior high, teachers write notes on the board to help students learn skills in taking notes and in organizing what is given orally. Through these processes, it is assumed that students will learn to listen more accurately and to evaluate information. This support is often not provided at the senior high level, the college level, or beyond in the "work world" of adults.

For some individuals, the retention of information heard develops without additional assistance. However, there are some for whom retention of auditory information is very difficult and others who once had listening skills but lost them through neurological disease or accident. Difficulties may arise in retaining facts; attaching meaning to information; identifying, abstracting, and integrating major ideas; and identifying transition statements. Researchers argue that some of the comprehension difficulties of children with specific language impairment are influenced by a limited capacity memory system (Carpenter, Just, and Shell, 1990; Lahey and Bloom, 1994) or by how well these children manage their limited working memory systems (Montgomery, 1996). These difficulties may affect academic skills such as note taking, test performance, and recall of information, and also daily living skills like taking phone messages and following conversations within groups. In addition, individuals may become confused during discussions and/or have difficulty following oral directions. These listening and recalling difficulties may lead to frustration, poor self-image, and poor performance at school or in a job. These individuals need special help to listen more effectively to auditory information, and they need unique resources, such as *Listen and Recall: Memory Strategies for Adolescents and Adults,* to develop improved memory skills.

Goal of **Listen and Recall**

The overall goal of *Listen and Recall: Memory Strategies for Adolescents and Adults* is to improve auditory attention and memory during listening. *Memory* is defined as the storage (encoding), retention, and recall of information. *Listening* is defined as the reception and comprehension of oral information through the aural modality. *Listen and Recall* is designed for use with individuals who have auditory memory deficits and/or ineffective listening and memory strategies. This resource helps these individuals develop strategies for the storage, retention, and recall of information presented orally, so that they will improve their listening in daily, personal, academic, and vocational situations. *Listen and Recall* can be effective both with individuals who have never had adequate listening skills (e.g., due to a learning disability) and those who once had the skills but lost them (e.g., due to a brain injury).

Intended Population

Listen and Recall is well suited for adolescents (i.e., those 11 years of age or older) and adults. It can be effective with normally achieving students, those who have language and/or learning disabilities, and those who present with neurological impairments.

Although the process is not fully understood, it is agreed that short-term memory has a limited capacity that increases throughout childhood. In contrast to older children, younger children use more passive rote memorization (Folds, Footo, Guttentag, and Ornstein, 1990). As children's knowledge increases and they become more efficient in their thinking, less mental effort is required (Bjorklund, Muir-Broaddus, and Schneider, 1990).

By the age of 11 or 12, youngsters have developed skills, language, and knowledge that free up space in their short-term memories (Naito and Komatsu, 1993). At these ages and older, they are more able to use this space for memory strategies. They demonstrate greater organizational skills, have more active integration with existing knowledge, transfer strategies to other situations, and can reflect on strategies they are taught (Folds et al., 1990; Schneider and Pressley, 1989).

Both normally achieving students and those with learning disabilities profit from the use of memory strategies. Although knowledge of strategies increases with age, even successful learners (e.g., college students) may have limited knowledge of effective memory strategies (Schneider and Pressley, 1989). Individuals with learning disabilities have less elaborate rehearsal strategies, are slower at naming and retrieving semantic information, and do not shift readily from using visual attributes to using semantic attributes (Lorsbach and Gray, 1985).

People who have experienced brain injuries often require retraining in memory strategies. However, rehearsal, attention, and concentration are necessary to successfully master this retraining (Parenté and Herrmann, 1996). Therefore, the individual must be able to attend and concentrate reasonably well and must be able to use rehearsal to remember information before he or she can relearn the memory strategies described in *Listen and Recall.*

Note that *Listen and Recall* relies on mental imagery as a memory strategy. Imagery may not be a viable method for individuals with residual right hemisphere lesions (Parenté and Herrmann, 1996). However, imagery is effective and useful for survivors of brain injury who have made gains in recovery.

Settings for Using Listen and Recall

These materials can be used in several settings by a variety of professionals. Any setting in which adolescents or adults are seen for language remediation (e.g., schools, hospitals, clinics, and private practices) will be appropriate for *Listen and Recall.* Since speech-language pathologists are well versed in diagnosing and remediating auditory deficits, these materials will be an excellent resource for them. Other professionals who may find these materials useful include learning disabilities specialists, rehabilitation team members, and educators whose focus is on language, listening, or study skills.

To be effective with individuals who have memory deficits, this program must be used in full, beginning with Section I and continuing through Section IV, until there is evidence that these strategies are being applied habitually. This requires a regular time commitment. In the school setting, this is more likely to be accomplished in remedial sessions or in a regular class that focuses on a broad range of study strategies. In a clinic or hospital setting, it might be accomplished in individual or small-group sessions and with assigned practice between sessions. Family members might be enlisted to observe the intervention sessions and to direct practice exercises.

In some school settings, especially in the areas of mathematics, science, English, and social studies, there is pressure to cover specific curricular content within a limited time, leaving little time for topics other than the subject matter. However, when an inclusive educational model is used, such classes provide an opportunity for generalizing use of memory strategies or for teaching students who do not have significant deficits but who lack experience with these strategies. Suggestions throughout this resource encourage generalization to the classroom setting.

Listen and Recall is designed for flexibility. Materials may be used in sessions with one individual, a small group, or a large group (e.g., in a classroom). Also, *Listen and Recall* may be used as one component in a broader program to improve listening skills. Such a program may include, among other areas, the skills of comprehension, critical listening, and appreciative listening. Adolescent or adult students can be taught to listen for the organization of lectures, and main and supporting ideas. They may be taught to ask questions for clarification and to take notes (Alley and Deshler, 1979). Adults can be taught to listen for main ideas during a news program and to follow oral directives that they might hear from their doctors or employers.

Assumptions Underlying *Listen and Recall*

Memory has been studied extensively, and yet those studies are generally far removed from educational practices (Neisser and Winograd, 1988). This presents a challenge to those who have the responsibility of providing remediation. *Listen and Recall* provides practical methods and materials that reflect current research and theory.

Listen and Recall is based on three underlying assumptions. The first is that memory can be improved by the use of memory strategies. Using these strategies requires effort. They may be applied consciously and are goal directed (Ashcraft, 1990; Bjorklund and Harnishfeyer, 1990; Bjorklund, Muir-Broaddus, and Schneider, 1990; Pressley, Symons, Snyder, and Cariglia-Bull, 1989). Even experienced and successful students are often inefficient strategy users (Schneider and Pressley, 1989). A language disability or learning disability can further affect the use and learning of strategies (Deshler, Schumaker, and Lenz, 1984b). Individuals may lack strategies and need to be taught how to reflect on their own cognitive processes (Swanson, 1990).

The second assumption is closely related to the first. To be recalled, information must be rehearsed, encoded, then stored (Parenté and Herrmann, 1996). Through rehearsal, one can maintain information so that it can be encoded (processed more deeply) using, for example, interpretation, expansion, and organization (Kirchner and Klatzky, 1985). When individuals use strategies, they are moving information into deeper levels of memory where it can be stored and later recalled. Encoding is critical for remembering information long term and retrieving it efficiently (Parenté and Herrmann, 1996). Individuals with and without learning disabilities, and with and without brain injuries, profit from processing at deeper levels (Harrell, Parenté, Bellingrath, and Lisicia, 1992; Schneider and Pressley, 1989; Walker and Poteet, 1989).

The third assumption underlying *Listen and Recall* is that memory improves when listeners are actively involved in mentally processing the information. By developing memory strategies, individuals become active learners. Annett (1995) quoted several studies demonstrating that subtle motor activities are supportive of memory and that when these motor activities are disrupted, memory is affected. For example, when articulation was suppressed, verbal memory was disrupted. When there was interference with voluntary eye movements, visuospatial imagery was disrupted. This strongly suggests that active involvement is important in memory processes.

Especially for individuals with brain injuries, strategies for mentally processing information is important. Simple mental exercises, as provided by stimulation therapy, do not improve memory because no new learning or new ways to process information take place, and the exercises tend to provide an environment for individuals to practice remembering using their inefficient memory methods (Crosson and Buenning, 1984; Dansereau, 1985; Godfrey and Knight, 1988).

Identifying Individuals with Inefficient Memory Strategies

Informal Indicators

Individuals with auditory memory deficits during listening can be identified formally and informally. These deficits can affect both behavior and performance. A list of informal indicators to identify individuals who could benefit from development of memory strategies follows:

1. poor recall of names, numbers (Wiig and Semel, 1980), new information, or important details (Wood, 1982);

2. poor recall or confusion of oral directions at school (Rampp, 1980; Wiig and Semel, 1980), at home, or on the job (Wiig and Semel, 1980);

3. frustration when required to recall information (Wiig and Semel, 1980);

4. confusion over the sequence of directions (Wiig and Semel, 1980);

5. inconsistent work due to the confusion and chaos of perceptions (Rampp, 1980) or because previously learned information is not recalled (Wood, 1982);

6. slow learning of information, although the quality of the learning may be high (Bryan and Bryan, 1978);

7. note taking that is limited in quality and quantity;

8. discrepancy between achievement scores and classwork/homework, or discrepancy between classwork and test scores (Wood, 1982);

9. difficulty adhering to classroom rules and etiquette, although basically compliant (Wood, 1982);

10. excessive quietness or passivity (Wood, 1982);

11. tendency to cover up failure by cheating or lying (Wood, 1982);

12. greater success on conceptual aspects of the curriculum as compared with schoolwork that requires memorization (Adams and Sheslow, 1990);

13. low motivation (Adams and Sheslow, 1990); and

14. greater skills in reading comprehension than listening comprehension, especially at younger ages (Carlisle, 1990).

The above information has been incorporated into two checklists. Professionals providing intervention in a school setting might use Appendix A: *Checklist of Informal Indicators of Memory—Version 1* to solicit information from teachers about an adolescent or adult student. Professionals providing intervention to adults in a clinic or hospital setting might use Appendix B: *Checklist of Informal Indicators of Memory—Version 2* to solicit information from family members and/or colleagues.

Formal Indicators

"Memory is a key feature of human intelligence in many respects" (Reynolds and Bigler, 1994, p. 1). In spite of its importance and maybe due to its complexity, terminology in defining memory can be confusing. It is important to have some guidelines in identifying auditory memory problems.

The following formal indicators might be used to identify individuals with auditory memory deficits who could benefit from *Listen and Recall*. It is acknowledged that tests measuring memory have been found to be poorly correlated with each other (Ceci, Ringstrom, and Lea, 1981) and that research on memory is fraught with many problems (Eysenck, 1977). However, formal tests can be informative when used cautiously and when the results are analyzed carefully. The tasks themselves vary greatly in syntactic content, length of stimuli, cognitive challenges inherent in the task, semantic content, presence or absence of visual stimuli, type of response required, whether repetition is allowed in presenting the oral stimuli, and even whether stimuli are presented by the examiner or by audio recording. Two subtests may have the same title, for example, the Oral Directions subtest of the *DTLA–2* and the Oral Directions subtest of the *CELF–R,* yet they are different tasks and yield very different results for the same individual. These subtests vary in visual stimuli presented and in response required, and they present different challenges for the test taker.

Test scores provide only an indication of success at performing a task. The examiner can supplement that information with extension testing, observation, or diagnostic teaching. For instance, if someone asks for many items to be repeated, the examiner can note that there may be an auditory memory problem and explore this possibility following the testing. Additionally, diagnostic information is available from the reports of other diagnosticians. The following formal tests and subtests include an auditory memory component. Although these tests should be administered only by persons trained to administer them (e.g., psychologists are trained to administer intelligence tests), the information below can be helpful in understanding the tests that yielded the scores. Although some of these instruments are out of print, they may still be used by examiners and so are included here.

1. *Wechsler Intelligence Scale for Children–Revised (WISC–R)* (Wechsler, 1974); *WISC–III* (Wechsler, 1991); and *Wechsler Adult Intelligence Scale–Revised (WAIS–R)* (Wechsler, 1981). Norms are provided from 6;0 years to 16;11 years for the *WISC–R* and *WISC–III,* and from 16 years to 74 years for the *WAIS–R.*

   a. Digit Span—A series of digits are presented orally. The listener repeats them forward and backward. The subtest measures immediate recall of digit series forward and backward.

   b. Arithmetic—Arithmetic problems are presented orally and solved mentally. The subtest measures retaining and processing word problems presented orally.

2. *Wide Range Assessment of Memory and Learning (WRAML)* (Adams and Sheslow, 1990). Norms are provided from 5;0 years through 17;11 years.

The *WRAML* yields a Verbal Memory Index based on three subtests, which can be compared with a Visual Memory Index and a Learning Index. A Learning Scale can be calculated which includes one verbal, one visual, and one cross-modal task. The following comprise the verbal memory subtests:

a. Number/Letter Memory—Random lists of numbers and letters mixed together are presented orally. The individual repeats them.

b. Sentence Memory—Sentences of increasing length are presented orally. The listener repeats them verbatim.

c. Story Memory—Two stories are read aloud. The individual retells the stories. A Delayed Recall trial for each story is possible. Recall can also be measured using a Recognition Task for story memory. Questions are asked about parts of the story that the individual did not recall spontaneously.

d. Verbal Learning—Up to 16 nonrelated words are presented orally. The listener immediately repeats as many as possible. Three additional presentation/recall trials follow. A Delayed Trial administration allows for observation of delayed recall.

3. *Test of Memory and Learning (TOMAL)* (Reynolds and Bigler, 1994). Norms are provided from 5;0 years to 9;11 years. The *TOMAL* consists of 10 subtests (5 verbal and 5 nonverbal) which are divided into a Verbal Memory Scale and a Nonverbal Memory Scale. There are four supplementary subtests, of which three are verbal. Calculating a Delayed Recall Index is also possible. The following are the verbal subtests that require auditory memory:

a. Memory for Stories—Short stories are presented orally followed immediately by a retelling of the story by the listener. A trial for delayed recall is possible.

b. Word Selective Reminding—A list of up to 12 words is presented orally and then is repeated by the listener. The individual hears the words that he or she omitted and repeats the entire list for as many as eight trials. The sequence of words repeated is unimportant. A trial for delayed recall is possible.

c. Digits Forward—Sets of from 2 to 10 numbers are presented orally. The listener repeats them in the order presented.

d. Paired Recall—Six or eight word pairs are presented orally. Then the first word in each pair is presented. The individual must give the word that was paired with the first word. Four trials are presented.

   e. Digits Backward—Sets of from two to nine numbers are presented orally. The listener repeats them in reverse order.

4. *Woodcock-Johnson Psycho-Educational Battery–Revised: Tests of Cognitive Ability (WJ–R)* (Woodcock and Johnson, 1989, 1990). Norms are provided from 2;0 years to 90+ years.

   a. Memory for Names—The listener is shown a picture of a space creature and told the creature's name (which is an entirely unfamiliar one- to three-syllable word). The listener then chooses the creature from a display of nine others. Additional names and creatures are added until nine names have been learned in this manner. Corrections are provided when errors are made. Long-term name retrieval is evaluated in this test. Delayed recall testing is optional from one to eight days later.

   b. Memory for Sentences—Oral presentations increase from single words to sentences that become increasingly more complex in syntax, vocabulary, and context. The simplest items are presented by the examiner. Presentation of the more difficult items is made by use of a tape recording, although presentation by the examiner is an option. The individual repeats the sentences verbatim.

   c. Memory for Words—Lists of up to eight words are presented orally on a tape recording, although presentation by the examiner is an option. The listener repeats the stimuli in the order presented.

   d. Numbers Reversed—A list of up to eight numbers is presented orally. The listener is asked to repeat them backward. Easier sets are presented by the examiner. Longer sets are presented by use of a tape recording, although presentation by the examiner is an option.

   e. Listening Comprehension—Taped passages are presented. The listener is asked to supply the word missing at the end of the passage. Oral presentation by the examiner is also an option.

5. *Clinical Evaluation of Language Fundamentals–Revised (CELF–R)* (Semel, Wiig, Secord, and Sabers, 1987) and *CELF–3* (Semel, Wiig, and Secord, 1995). Norms are provided from 5;0 years to 16;0 years for the *CELF–R* and from 6;0 years to 21;11 years for the *CELF–3*.

   a. Semantic Relationships *(CELF–R, CELF–3)*—Questions are presented orally. The relationships include comparative, spatial, passive, and temporal, and a fifth relationship, sequential, is included in the *CELF–3.* The listener responds by choosing two answers out of the four options printed in the stimulus book. Repetition of the question is allowed without penalty.

b. Oral Directions *(CELF–R, CELF–3)*—Oral directions of one, two, or three commands are presented orally with up to three modifiers. Serial orientation and left/right orientation are included. Visual stimuli are present during the presentation and response. The listener identifies the correct geometrical form(s). The subtests measure interpreting, recalling, and executing oral commands.

c. Concepts and Directions *(CELF–3)*—Oral directions of one, two, or three commands are presented orally with increasing length and complexity. Linguistic concepts such as *all, none, except, farthest,* and *neither* are included.

d. Listening to Paragraphs *(CELF–R, CELF–3)*—Paragraphs of increasing length and complexity are presented orally. The listener answers questions about the information. The subtest measures recall of information presented orally. Two paragraphs are available for each age level. Questions require recall of information, identification of cause-effect relationships, inferences, and predictions. This subtest can be used to measure baseline performance and monitor progress for *Listen and Recall* strategies.

e. Recalling Sentences *(CELF–R, CELF–3)*—Sentences of varying length and syntactic complexity are presented orally. Listeners repeat them verbatim.

f. Word Classes *(CELF–R, CELF–3)*—Three to four words are presented orally. Repetition of stimulus words is not allowed. The listener chooses the two words that go together best. In the *CELF–R,* the categories include semantic class, opposites, spatial, and temporal, and in the *CELF–3,* they include antonyms, part-whole relationships, semantic class, and synonyms.

6. *Test of Adolescent and Adult Language (TOAL–3)* (Hammill, Brown, Larsen, and Wiederholt, 1987). Norms are provided from 12;0 years through 24;11 years.

a. Listening/Grammar—Three sentences are read aloud. The listener chooses the two sentences that mean the same thing. All three sentences can be repeated once.

b. Speaking/Grammar—Sentences are read aloud. The listener repeats them verbatim. A sentence can be repeated after the test is completed.

7. *Detroit Tests of Learning Aptitude (DTLA)* (Baker and Leland, 1967); *DTLA–2* (Hammill, 1985); *DTLA–3* (Hammill, 1991); *Detroit Tests of Learning Aptitude–Adult (DTLA–A)* (Hammill and Bryant, 1991). Norms are provided from 6;0 years to 17;0 years for the *DTLA*, the *DTLA–2*, and the *DTLA–3*, and from 16;0 years to 79;11 years for the *DTLA–A*.

   a. Auditory Attention Span for Unrelated Words *(DTLA);* retitled Word Sequences in *DTLA–2, DTLA–3,* and *DTLA–A* — Lists of two to eight words are presented orally. The listener repeats as many of them as possible. The subtests measure immediate recall of series of unrelated words. In the *DTLA–2* and *DTLA–3,* three to eight words are presented; in the *DTLA–A,* three to six words are presented. *DTLA–3* and *DTLA–A* have a few additional items.

   b. Auditory Attention Span for Related Syllables *(DTLA);* retitled Sentence Imitation in *DTLA–2, DTLA–3,* and *DTLA–A*— Sentences of increasing length are presented orally. The listener repeats them verbatim. The subtests measure immediate recall and repetition of sentences. In the *DTLA–2,* Hammill (1985) describes this as a "measure of grammar usage" (p. 5) rather than a test of memory. In the *DTLA–3,* the sentences have been revised to "make the subtest more clearly a measure of grammar usage" (Hammill, 1991, p. 10). In the *DTLA–A,* the administration and scoring have also been revised to be "a measure of auditory memory relating to spoken syntax and grammar" (Hammill and Bryant, 1991, p. 10).

   c. Oral Directions *(DTLA* and *DTLA–2);* not included in *DTLA–3*—Directions of increasing length are presented orally. The listener performs them on a page of visual-graphic symbols. This subtest measures retaining, recalling, and performing oral directions of increasing difficulty with a visual component present.

   d. Reversed Letters *(DTLA–3* and *DTLA–A)*—Series of two to eight letter names are presented orally. The listener writes the letters in reverse order. This subtest is a measure of auditory memory for spoken letters, as well as for spatial ability and for eye-hand coordination.

   e. Mathematical Problems *(DTLA–A)*—Mathematical word problems are presented orally. The listener solves them mentally.

   f. Basic Information (*DTLA–A*)—Questions about basic information are presented orally and answered orally.

8. *The Learning and Memory Battery (LAMB)* (Schmidt and Tombaugh, 1995). Norms are provided from age 20 years through 80 years.

a. Paragraph Learning—A nonthematic paragraph with 31 facts is presented. This subtest measures free and cued recall following two learning trials.

b. Word List Learning—A 15-word list is presented with five learning trials. Free and cued recall are measured.

c. Word Pair Learning—Fourteen word pairs are presented following four learning trials. Word pairs are recalled in a delayed recall and recognition trials.

d. Digit Span and Supraspan Learning—Digit span recall forward and backward are measured in this subtest. Four learning trials are presented followed by a supraspan learning task and a supraspan relearning task the following day.

Description of *Listen and Recall* Sections

Listen and Recall progresses through four phases, each represented by a section:

1. retention and recall of spoken unrelated words (Section I);

2. retention and recall of spoken facts (Section II);

3. retention and recall of information in spoken articles (Section III); and

4. retention and recall of oral directions (Section IV).

Within this resource, activities progress from an emphasis on retention of unrelated semantic units not embedded in a syntactic structure to retention of lengthy information with complex syntactic structure. In the first phase, Section I, listeners learn to make imaginative associations and to use visualization to aid memory and recall. Listeners initially make drawings of the unrelated words to facilitate the visualization strategy they are learning. In the second phase, Section II, listeners are taught to use association and visualization to recall facts that include names of people, places, and things, and numerical information.

After acquiring these strategies, listeners learn to recall information they might hear in a discussion, lecture, or news report. Such activities comprise Section III. In addition to association and visualization, the use of other memory strategies (i.e., kinesthetic imagery, counting, rehearsal, key words, organization, asking for repetition, and knowledge base) is encouraged in this third phase. In the fourth phase, Section IV, listeners recall oral directions using these same memory strategies and two more memory strategies are suggested: wh-questions and eliminating distractions.

Descriptions and the rationale of each phase are given at the beginning of each section. An elaborate description of the *Listen and Recall* method is presented in the introduction to Section I. Sentence complexity, vocabulary level, sophistication of content, and idea density have been controlled when possible throughout the activities. The interplay of these factors is quite complex. Complete control of these factors in specific sentences is, however, beyond the scope of this resource and would require elaborate research. In Sections III and IV, which include materials that are paragraph length and longer, the most difficult types of sentences are excluded, since the purpose of these materials is to teach a method of listening and not to teach syntactic skills.

Using *Listen and Recall*

Order of Presentation

Listen and Recall Section I should be presented first; next Section II should be presented with occasional review of Section I; then Sections III and IV should follow, overlapping in presentation, and with reviews of Sections I and II as needed. This sequence is represented in Figure 1. The period of presentation for each section is represented by the gray bar moving through time from left to right.

Figure 1

PRESENTATION ORDER OF SECTIONS

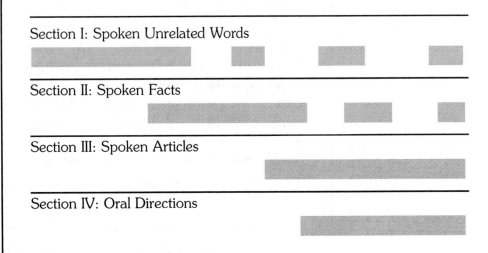

Section I: Spoken Unrelated Words

Section II: Spoken Facts

Section III: Spoken Articles

Section IV: Oral Directions

Period of Time Required

The length of time needed to teach the memory strategies is related to each individual's needs and motivation. Memory strategies are not completely developed until they are generalized into daily situations outside of the setting where they are learned. There is little point in teaching a memory strategy unless it is used in daily life situations. One student with whom this author worked, who was particularly capable and motivated, experienced positive changes in her listening within a few months. Other students, who were motivated but had greater difficulties, continued to make steady progress after two years. As a general rule, individuals should receive 20 to 30 minutes of listening and memory strategy remediation individually or in a group two times a week until strategies have generalized to relevant situations.

Directions to the Adult Providing Intervention

The directions for teaching recall strategies are presented at the beginning of each section. Each section builds on the preceding section; therefore, directions for all sections should be read before using the materials. Section I includes directions and suggestions that are basic to all the sections following. They are the key to teaching the *Listen and Recall* strategies; therefore, it is important to read through Section I especially carefully. The term *adult providing intervention* will be used throughout the book, although other terms such as *speech-language pathologist, special educator,* or *rehabilitation specialist* also would have been appropriate.

Writing Goals and Objectives

On an educational or rehabilitational plan, the general goal for listeners using *Listen and Recall* could be to improve auditory memory during listening tasks. However, more specific goals are given at the beginning of each section. For adults providing intervention in a school setting, these goals are appropriate for use in developing and implementing individualized educational programs (IEPs). The goals allow flexibility in choosing the rate and direction of the progression within a given period of time. To use the goals stated in each section to write objectives, add measurable information based on each individual's needs. Examples follow:

   I. Goal: The listener will recall unrelated words presented orally.

     Short-term Objective: Given 10 unrelated words presented orally, the listener will recall them with 80 percent success.*

    * Usually, 10 words is a comfortable goal for individuals to recall with 80 percent accuracy. If an individual has unusually severe memory difficulties, decrease the number of words presented.

II. Goal: The listener will recall facts from a paragraph presented orally.

Short-term Objective: Given 8 facts from an oral presentation, the listener will recall them with 80 percent accuracy.

III. Goal: The listener will recall facts from an article presented orally.

Short-term Objective: Given an orally presented article of 25 facts, the listener will recall the facts with 75 percent accuracy.

IV. Goal: The listener will recall oral directions.

Short-term Objective: Given oral directions containing 10 points of information, the listener will recall the information with 80 percent success.

Rate of Presentation

Materials are presented at the speed that is comfortable to the listener and at a speed that supports success. Pausing between facts when necessary is helpful. Discussing and supporting the memory strategies should be done as needed. With practice, the use of strategies will become more automatic and habitual. As this occurs, the listener will need less time to process and less support in strategy use. Support is gradually withdrawn until the listener is successful without it.

Orienting Schema

Knowledge about a topic is a strong factor in successful recall (Schneider and Pressley, 1989). Neisser (1976) refers to this knowledge as built from experiences of the past and refers to it as *schema.* When this knowledge is activated, it helps orient listeners to the information to be presented.

When listeners in any situation have no orienting schema, the initial moments of listening are spent becoming oriented to the topic and to the style of the presentation. Since this can affect memory, the adult providing intervention will want to spend time orienting the listener before actually implementing the lesson.

This parallels the process that occurs in reading whereby the more background knowledge regarding the topic the reader brings to the reading task, the better the comprehension and recall of the information read. This, of course, is a basic tenet of the whole language approach to reading instruction in which readers participate in a good deal of "prereading" activities designed to increase their knowledge base about the information prior to engaging in the actual reading.

In Section II of *Listen and Recall,* the illustration and title are helpful in orienting the listener to the topic. In Sections III and IV, in addition to the title of the presentation, suggestions are often given to orient the listener to the information about to be presented.

Motivating Participants and Monitoring Progress

Interest and motivation are important elements in all teaching activities but particularly in memory strategy development. Without interest and motivation, there is little learning and even less use of the strategies in novel situations. For some individuals, there is an internal motivation that may involve the desire to learn, natural curiosity, or the desire to please. This internal motivation will continue as they learn listening and memory strategies. For others, the successes they experience in using these materials will motivate them to practice the strategies.

Keeping individuals motivated is usually easy during the initial stages of *Listen and Recall* because the activities are perceived as fun. Participants like the naturally creative elements in the memory strategies being taught. They may enjoy the drawings; they may enjoy the absurd associations. Also, for a high percentage of individuals, there is immediate, demonstrable improvement in memory skills.

As discussed, *Listen and Recall* is structured around progressive objectives. Use the objectives to motivate individuals toward success. Discuss the objectives and the progression necessary to achieve them. Keep individual progress sheets on each participant so he or she can review personal successes. Appendix C presents a blank *Progress Sheet* that can duplicated and used to record objectives and to document progress toward meeting them. Figure 2 on the next page illustrates a completed *Progress Sheet,* including name, date, lesson presented, and results. Comments can be added by the participant or by the adult providing intervention. Comments can list specific strategies used and whether they were successful, or they can include information about generalizing to other situations. Comments can be as general or specific as is helpful.

The adult providing intervention might also elect to use the *Steps to Success* monitoring sheet, on which a drawing of stairs represents the four sections and goals. The first step is recall for words, the second is paragraphs, and the third and fourth are articles and oral directions.

Figure 2
EXAMPLE COMPLETED PROGRESS SHEET

Progress Sheet

Name *Stu*   Date *2/3*

Date	Presentation	Results	Comments
2/5	7 words	4/7	no strategies used
	10 words w/ drawing	10/10	applied strategies w/ help
	10 words w/ drawing	10/10	applied strategies w/ help
2/10	12 words w/ drawing	12/12	applied strategies w/o help
	10 words w/ drawing	10/10	applied strategies w/o help
	12 words w/o drawing	12/12	association done orally as a group
2/17	10 words w/o drawing	8/10	created association orally independently
	10 words w/o drawing	7/10	created association silently, independently,, applied strategies w/o help
2/24	card #1	7/10	applied strategies w/ help, we talked it through
	card #2	13/14	applied strategies independently w/o help
2/29	card #3	—	reported he couldn't concentrate today
3/4	card #4	10/12	reviewed strategies first, some help for focus
	card #5	16/16	good associations today
3/6	card #6	9/10	good associations today
	card #7	8/16	no associations made; needed to concentrate more
3/11	card #8	10/10	well done w/ help
	card #9	8/13	62% w/o help
3/13	card #10	10/17	w/o help
	card #11	12/15	worked on #s
3/18	card #12	12/13	shared that he is trying to use strategies in social studies class
	card #13	12/13	92% w/o help
3/20	May Pierstorff	15/19	names difficult, practiced associations
	Early Planes	12/14	picturing the action helped, recalled 6 facts spontaneously, 6 w/?'s

Figure 3
EXAMPLE COMPLETED STEPS TO SUCCESS

Steps to Success

Name *John*   Date *10/21*

Oral Directions

Date begun: *1/31*

Date completed: _____

Articles

Date begun: *1/21*

Date completed: _____

Paragraphs

Date begun: *11/21*

Date completed: *1/15*

makes excellent associations

is 85% accurate recalling facts from paragraphs

Words

Date begun: *10/21*

Date completed: *11/15*

is 90% accurate recalling 10 words

Explain to the participants that when they have completed all steps, they will have developed effective memory strategies and will have had much practice in applying them. Appendix D includes a blank *Steps to Success* form that may be duplicated. Figure 3 displays this form as it might be completed.

With some students, this author has used the analogy of a foundation for a house, which was drawn on the students' progress sheets when explaining that they were learning the foundation of memory. Using the strategies in *Listen and Recall,* they would eventually add walls, a roof, and other elements to construct a whole house as they progressed from using illustrations to recalling information mentally. Since the foundation and house were drawn on their individual progress sheets on which their successes were recorded, they were referred to whenever it was helpful to remind students of their goals.

Developing short-term objectives and motivating on a day-to-day basis can also be very helpful. Some listeners may expect to perform perfectly, and when others get perfect scores, they may compare themselves negatively. It is helpful to set an achievable objective such as, "I have given you 10 words. If you can recall 8, I will know this strategy is working for you." With use of the strategies developed in *Listen and Recall,* most listeners will recall 8 words and then feel accomplished if they recall more than that. Point out that achieving 80 percent accuracy is adequate. Those who have difficulty reaching 80 percent recall for words may need extra help in making stronger associations (i.e., more active, absurd associations).

When internal motivation to improve is not strong enough, external incentives may be needed. For some younger adolescents, points can be used to motivate performance. When they are tallied on progress sheets, they provide a source of pride each time progress is reviewed. Points can also be used to gain tangible items such as stickers or other treats.

For some adolescent students, the prospect of learning strategies to help them get better grades on tests will be motivating. Some individuals may be interested to know that entertainers who perform memory feats on stage can use similar strategies to remember 100 words yelled to them from the audience—and that when someone in the audience asks such an entertainer to give the 45th word or the 78th word, he or she can do it. The performer could even give words 85 down to 75, in that order, if asked. That's how strong the strategies can be!

For adolescents and adults with brain injury, monetary incentives have dramatically improved memory and learning (Parenté and Herrmann, 1996). According to Parenté and Herrmann (1996), this is not true for persons without brain injury. Monetary incentives for non-brain-injured individuals improves learning (i.e., more effort is exerted), but not remembering (i.e., there is less effect on long-term memory).

Some listeners enjoy the drawings done in Section I so much that they resist moving to the steps that require no drawing. Several tactics may help in this transition. Again, explaining the objectives and the steps can be helpful. Examples of others who have succeeded previously can be shared as long as privacy is respected (e.g., "I have a student who just finished this program, and in the beginning he could only remember 4 out of 7 words, but by the time he had practiced recalling words, paragraphs, and articles, he could remember as many as 30 facts. You will be so proud of yourself when your memory strategies are that effective"). For some, a gradual withdrawal from the use of illustrations works well (e.g., "You can draw an illustration after you do two sets of words without illustrations").

An effective way to make the transition from words to paragraphs is to ask listeners for names of favorite teachers or people from their past. Then practice using absurd associations and images to recall the names. The names of performers or sports figures can be used as well.

Not only is it appropriate for family members to be informed of progress, it can also be a great motivator. When family members learn about the successes of the participant, they provide reinforcement, and this influences the satisfaction the individual feels with his or her learning. On occasion, this author has photocopied an illustration or article, made a note regarding a participant's progress on the photocopy, and shared it with family members to show the student's success. A phone call home is another way to make this positive connection with family members, as is an invitation to observe sessions directly to become involved in the process.

If listeners insist that their method (e.g., rehearsal) works better and that they don't need "a trick," you can avoid some difficulty by affirming the importance of rehearsal as a technique. Rehearsal does help to keep words in short-term memory. However, *Listen and Recall* emphasizes strategies for long-term memory that will last longer. Compare the strategies by presenting lists of different lengths and having participants recall the lists first using rehearsal and then using another memory strategy. The next session, ask participants to recall the lists; compare their performance between strategies. Delayed recall can also be a definitive test of the strength of using strategies, because the associations and visualizations provide a stronger, deeper processing that yields improved memory and recall.

Generalization

One should not assume that generalization of a new strategy is automatic. Knowledge of a strategy does not guarantee its use (Deshler, Schumaker, and Lenz, 1984b). Generalization is enhanced by initially setting objectives with individuals based on awareness of their current habits, using practical activities including examples relevant to various situations, and encouraging application in other settings that may involve other professionals and family members (Deshler, Schumaker, and Lenz, 1984a; Parenté and Herrmann, 1996; Schneider and Pressley, 1989). The following steps are suggested to ensure generalization:

1. be direct and explicit about strategies, explaining each step fully;

2. model the strategies in many settings, with different conditions and with different people;

3. help participants assess their own gains; and

4. provide extensive practice, to gradually allow each individual to gain control of strategies.

The first two steps provide experience with strategy use. The last two build knowledge about one's own memory strategies (metamemory skills). Generalization occurs when individuals know when and where to use their strategies (Schneider and Pressley, 1989).

Pressley, Forest-Pressley, Elliott-Faust, and Miller (1985) suggest that the following metamemory skills are important. Users must recognize:

1. to which materials the strategies can be applied;

2. which goals can be met using the strategy;

3. the time constraints of the strategy;

4. the effort required to use the strategy;

5. what personal satisfaction can be derived from the strategy; and

6. how to modify the strategy.

The variety of materials and the generalization activities in Sections III and IV provide ample opportunity to develop metamemory skills. Discussion of strategy use in a variety of settings and for a variety of purposes is encouraged throughout *Listen and Recall*. As listening and memory strategies are taught and practiced, individuals can evaluate their goals and derive personal satisfaction from their achievements. As the adult providing intervention works with these individuals and observes successes, modifications can be made based on what is effective and what is not.

Some individuals may have difficulty when attempting to generalize use of strategies. Pressley et al. (1985) proposed a model of "production deficiencies" that can provide helpful insights. Individuals may have "deficient strategies" because their knowledge of a strategy is incomplete or poorly integrated. Second, they may have "insufficient metamemory about strategies." This may be because they lack knowledge of how to apply the strategy to a variety of situations or how to modify the strategy to fit the task, or they may find the effort is too great, which affects motivation. Third, individuals may fail to monitor strategy use effectively. This is referred to as "flawed monitoring." They may have inadequate use of a selected strategy because they fail to switch strategies when one proves ineffective. A particular individual may have difficulty with one, two, or all three of the areas just noted. If a listener is having particular difficulty, the adult providing intervention can identify the area(s) of "production deficiency" and develop the deficient skill.

While it is important for participants to build knowledge about and skill with a variety of memory strategies, it is also important for these strategies to become useful in many real-life situations. However, as noted by Bjorklund, Muir-Broaddus, and Schneider (1990), conscious use of strategies may use a large part of the limited memory capacity to process information. For this reason, it is important for the strategies to become thoroughly practiced and automatic during listening.

Retention and Recall of Spoken Unrelated Words

Goal: The listener will recall unrelated words presented orally.

Rationale

Listen and Recall begins with this section titled "Retention and Recall of Spoken Unrelated Words." Although there are situations in which one has to recall a list of unrelated words (e.g., grocery items to buy), the author acknowledges that such listening activities are generally artificial and may be more difficult for impaired communicators to process than activities involving related words. However, Section I is the initial step in *Listen and Recall* for specific reasons that are unrelated to the application of these activities in daily life.

First, the simplicity of the materials in Section I enables the adult providing intervention to probe for existing listening and memory strategies that listeners already use. Second, since the exercises are relatively free of semantic and syntactic context, participants are able to concentrate on learning the strategies of visualization and association. If the exercises were presented in a semantic or syntactic context (such as factual information, sentences, or paragraphs), associations would be influenced and possibly restricted by the context. Exercises using unrelated words enable participants to associate more freely. For similar reasons, the simplicity of the materials in Section I enables the listeners to focus more easily on the strategy of visualizing. The strategy is then strengthened and generalized in the remaining three sections.

Beginning with unrelated words has several additional advantages. Because of the simplicity of the task, the requirements of the task remain fairly consistent from one presentation to another; therefore, progress is dramatic and easily demonstrated. An individual who recalls three to four words before using memory techniques will be recalling longer lists within a short time. He or she is quickly aware of the benefits of using memory strategies. Furthermore, in this section it is easy to demonstrate that words that have been forgotten have not been associated and visualized.

The assumption that visual imagery and association are successful strategies for recall of word lists is borne out by a study by Bower and Winzenz (1970). They compared recall of paired associates when four different instructions were given to the subjects: (1) to repeat the words silently, (2) to read aloud sentences containing the words, (3) to construct and read aloud sentences that associated the two words, and (4) to form an image in which the two words were in "vivid interaction." Recall was significantly greater for condition 4. Condition 3 was the next most effective, followed by 2, and then by 1. In another study, Bower (1970) reported that recall of information was considerably higher when subjects were instructed to form images that interact instead of forming separate images.

In their extensive review of research, Schneider and Pressley (1989) found evidence that association and other memory strategies can improve memory tremendously. Further, they state that "there are substantial associations between achievement and reported strategy use" (p. 162). Scruggs and Mastropieri (1989) found that students with learning disabilities dramatically benefited from associating words with pictures of acoustically similar words (e.g., alliance is like a lion making an agreement not to fight).

In investigating the use of imagery with survivors of brain injury, researchers have documented that training imagery is easier for recalling concrete items versus abstractions. They have also observed that imagery is most effective when the images actively interact (Higbee, 1988; McDaniel and Pressley, 1987; Richardson, 1992).

Word recall also has been found to be facilitated by depth of semantic analysis (Craik and Tulving, 1975; Jacoby, 1978; Moscovitch and Craik, 1976; Walsh and Jenkins, 1973). The following are examples of various depths of analysis:

1. shallow analysis—analysis of typeset information;

2. intermediate analysis—rhyming words; and

3. deep analysis—categorization (Craik and Tulving, 1975).

The deeper the analysis is, the greater the word recall. Other studies have reported that subjects involved in supplying part of the information to be remembered have greater recall than subjects who do not have that involvement (Donaldson and Boss, 1980; Jacoby, 1978; McFarland, Frey, and Rhodes, 1980; Slamecka and Graf, 1978).

In summary, the use of visual imagery (visualization) and association to recall information is supported by research. In addition, Section I of *Listen and Recall* (as well as the other sections) provides exercises in which conditions for recall are optimal, because listener involvement is high and depth of analysis is encouraged.

Presentation

This section, includes five steps that are sequenced to (1) orient listeners to *Listen and Recall* procedures, (2) assist in motivating them, (3) develop strategies for recalling unrelated words presented orally, and (4) provide practice using the strategies. In steps 1, 2, and 3, listeners learn strategies for recalling unrelated words by drawing them in association with one another. The first three steps are usually presented in one session. Step 3 is then practiced until the listener is highly successful, which commonly occurs in three to five sessions. In step 4, the adult providing intervention facilitates a transition from association in an illustration to visual mental images. This may require only one session if the listener is adept at visualization and associations. Several sessions will be necessary for some individuals whose associations are weaker and who find visualizing difficult. Step 5 requires completely independent visual imagery and associations without the use of illustrations. This step is practiced until the listener achieves the objective. Note that recall of no more than 6 unrelated words is needed to achieve adequate success, although recall of 10 unrelated words seems achievable for most participants.

Step 1: Introducing the Method

Present the following seven words orally and ask listeners to recall them. Increase interest by saying:

> "I am going to tell you seven words. Try to remember them. Remember as many as you can. Ready? *Dog, tail, mousetrap, chair, man, paint, cat.*"

(On the first presentation, say a new word about every two seconds.)

Have the listeners say (or write in the case of group presentations) as many of the words as they can, in any order. Record the number of words recalled for each participant and ask how each remembered the words. This reveals the participants' efficiency in using strategies and/or possible awareness of memory strategies (metamemory).

Read the following story and encourage listeners to run the story through their heads "like a movie" as it is told. Signal by raising a finger and counting each word from the list as the story is told:

"Picture a *dog*. He catches his *tail* in a *mousetrap*. He knocks over a *chair* with a *man* standing on it. The man spills *paint* on a *cat*."

Ask listeners to say (or write) the words again. At this point, encourage visualization and association (e.g., if a listener forgets the *chair*, ask what the *dog* does, or if the *cat* is forgotten, ask what happens to the *paint*). Participants usually can recall all *seven* words after the story is read. If seven words prove to be too challenging, start with three or four words and gradually add more.

This step usually convinces listeners that their memory will improve with visualization and association strategies. Point out their improved recall and how you will be helping them learn to use these strategies. Explain that these strategies will help them to remember things at school, on a job, and/or at home. Give relevant examples such as remembering names and dates in social studies, or recalling items to get at the grocery store.

Step 2: Demonstrating the Method

In this step, the adult providing intervention presents sets of illustrations to demonstrate visualization and association strategies. For this purpose, duplicate the *Illustrated Card Sets* in Appendix E onto heavy stock paper and cut apart to form cards. The *Illustrated Card Sets* are sequences of pictures representing unrelated words. Each consecutive card in a set has a single pictured word added. Card 1 of each set has two words illustrated, card 2 of each set has the first two illustrations and one additional illustration, card 3 adds one more, and so forth. The illustrations on the cards are drawn with simple unartistic style to demonstrate to participants that artistic ability is not important.

As an option, instead of using the illustrated cards, draw your own illustrations using words participants have selected. Verbalize a ridiculous, active association and draw an illustration with that association (e.g., a cow reading a book). This can perhaps add a good-natured laugh or two at your "artistic" ability, and the example sets up the situation in which the association, and not the art, is valued.

The Importance of Absurdity

The words to be recalled are unrelated and the associations are purposely ridiculous. Absurdity adds to retention. Point out absurdity to participants, and encourage them to use absurdities whenever their associations become mundane.

Presenting the Words

Beginning with Story 1, Card 1, present the two words orally, show the stimulus illustrations that portrays these words, and then read the association. Note that when you read the verbal association, the participants are no longer viewing the illustration. Present the next word from Card 2 and the illustration. Discuss the verbal association. Repeat this through Card 5.

If instead you are drawing the illustrations, select two words and then verbalize a ridiculous association. Draw the two illustrations on a blank card. (Using an overhead transparency also works well, especially in a group setting.) Choose additional words, one at a time, associating each to previous words. Add each word in that association to the drawing immediately after it is discussed.

Recalling the Words

When all six new words have been presented, turn over the illustrated cards so participants cannot see the illustrations and ask listeners to repeat (or write, in the case of a group) the words. If a participant is having difficulty, encourage the visual image and the verbal association by suggesting where or how the missing word was associated (e.g., "There was something on the piano. It came right after the knife. What did the kite do?"). Present three or more sets to demonstrate how visual images and associations are made.

Step 3: Practicing the Method with Drawings

After presenting three or more sets of examples, give the participants plain paper on which to draw their own associations. Say to them:

"Now *you* get a chance to make the associations. Remember to make each new word connect to the previous one in some active way, or in some absurd way. Make them *do* something together. It can be like a cartoon—anything is possible. You can have corn cobs turned into airplanes or dishes with ears. Anything goes."

Each participant will make different associations. The associations will be both visual and verbal, because the person is drawing and telling a storylike association.

Presenting the Words

Orally present up to 10 words from *Word List One* at the end of this section. Although fewer words can be presented to listeners with severe memory deficits, most are comfortable and successful with lists of 10 words. With the majority of participants, it is reasonable to ask them to recall 8 out of 10 words. More than 10 words in a list probably is not additionally productive. Occasionally, a participant may opt for 12 to 15 words or more. This can be time consuming but, if it aids motivation, it may be worth the time. Have participants add each illustration to the previous one. Present the words one at a time, slowly enough that listeners can complete their thinking processes, their associations, and their drawings but quickly enough that they must make simple drawings.

Lack of Artistic Ability

If participants are worried about artistic ability, reassure them by giving messages such as, "Don't worry about your drawings. This is not art class. This is for the purpose of improving your listening." Some individual's illustrations will not be recognizable. Figure 4 illustrates how three participants visualized and drew the words *fork, lightning, clock, dog, heart, peanut, bell, bridge, leaf,* and *swing*. The artistry varies, yet each illustration clearly made an association the participant remembered.

Some illustrations will be tiny. Do not judge them. However, discourage elaborate drawings because they slow the presentation of words and detract from the focus on auditory memory strategies.

Encouraging Imagination

Watch for participants piling things up in unrelated ways (e.g., the pea is on the pillow, the pillow is on the book, the cup is on the pillow) or using repetitive associations (e.g., the hammer hit the plane, the plane hit the balloon, the balloon hit the bee). *Active* associations are very important. The book could smash the pea all over the pillow and break the cup, or a cup of peas (with eyes) could be reading a book while sitting on a pillow, and so on. Encourage imagination!

Figure 4
PARTICIPANT ILLUSTRATIONS

Recalling the Words

After listeners have created their associations and drawings, have them turn over their papers before they repeat (or write) the words presented. They need not repeat words in the order of presentation. Recall is important, not order.

Follow-up

When a listener forgets a word, tell him or her the word and ask what the association was. When a word is forgotten, the association is usually weak. Discuss the necessity of strong associations. After listeners have recalled two or three sets of words, another option is to ask them to recall the words from the first set. They can usually remember them, and even partial recall is further proof to them of their ability to remember with this strategy.

Ask participants whether they visualized the items or used the associations to help recall the words. At first, both strategies should be encouraged, but eventually each participant will choose the one that fits his or her learning style. Continue this practice for three to four sessions or until participants are recalling 8 words out of a list of 10 with consistency.

Step 4: Internalizing the Visual Associations

Listeners next learn to make the associations between the orally presented words without an illustration. This can be done in a couple of ways. One way is for the participants to create an association together. Do this by choosing two words from *Word List One* at the end of this section. Tell a ridiculous, active association between the words. Choose another word and have a participant tell an association for the new word with the two previous words, and so on. This method presents an opportunity to model and encourage ridiculous but strong associations.

You might say:

"We are going to remember words without drawing them. We will take turns associating the words. The more ridiculous the associations, the better we will remember them. Remember to picture things happening as in a cartoon."

A second way of presenting this practice is to let participants take turns describing their own associations aloud for a whole set of words. Watch for participants who sometimes recall a related word instead of the given word (e.g., *clock* for *time,* because they have pictured a clock to represent *time,* or *knife* for *sharp,* because a knife was used to symbolize *sharp*). When this happens, teach the participant to watch for this error. Many can learn to recognize this potential problem as the association is made. The recognition facilitates more accurate recall.

Step 4 is complete when listeners make strong associations. This may be obvious after only a few sets, or it may take several sessions.

Step 5: Practicing Independent, Silent Associations

In this step, participants practice retaining and recalling words using visual imagery and association. Each participant independently associates the given words without the aid of illustrations or verbalizations.

Presenting the Words

Orally present words at the individual's pace. You can usually tell when participants are ready for the next word by a shift in their attention back to you as seen in eye contact. Participants compete only against themselves. Lists of words are provided beginning on page 35.

How Many Sets to Present

During any one session, participants will reach a saturation point. This may happen after as few as four sets of words. When this occurs, you will notice that an individual's success rate will decrease. Make a comment to this effect can be made to help participants be aware of their own memory processes:

"That's enough for today. If we do too many, they start to blend together. That's the way memory is. Short study periods are sometimes better than longer ones when there's much new information to memorize."

Follow-up

When a word is forgotten, determine which word it is and check the association that was made. Often it is a poorly associated word. Sometimes it is the last word presented and the listener did not take the time to associate it.

Individual Differences

Observe individual differences as participants learn to use the strategies in *Listen and Recall*. Although the strategies as presented are effective with a high percentage of participants who have listening and auditory memory deficits, individualization of the program may be advisable for some.

One student, for example, performed best when he did not visualize. For him, verbal association alone was a better approach for encoding and retrieval. This student was in a class with one other participant. Both were learning recall strategies for unrelated words. This particular student was very conscientious. However, his effort did not seem to improve his memory. When his use of association and visualization was probed to find out how he had encoded words, he was able to answer questions about how words were "connected" or what they "did to each other" (e.g., A hook was cooking a car on the stove), but he was very limited in his responses to what he had "pictured." When he was encouraged to use association without visualization, his performance improved.

Another student did exceptionally well using association and visualization for remembering unrelated words; however, her associations were unusually lengthy. This became a problem when she applied association to the facts in articles and oral directions because she required excessive amounts of time to encode information, and in the process of elaboration, she confused herself with unnecessary associations. Although she found the extensive associations to be pleasurable, her memory improvement was greatest when she was taught to use brief associations.

Period of Time

Continue Step 5 over a period of weeks until the desired improvement in auditory memory for unrelated words is achieved. Also work to increase the speed of recall, if possible, although this is not necessary. This last step in recall of unrelated words usually requires more sessions than the previous steps.

Difficulty with Section I does not necessarily mean that the participant cannot profit from the strategies presented. If progress is not seen, or it is very slow, move on to Section II, in which the approach is applied to more meaningful materials.

Suggestions for Generalization

After listeners have become comfortable using visualization, and absurd, active associations, try an activity that requires them to recall a name and other information associated with that name. By doing this, participants will begin to see the applicability of these techniques to their lives, which promotes generalizations and, helps them make the transition to Section II, "Retention and Recall of Spoken Facts." To do this activity and assist in this transition, be familiar with the strategies presented in Section II; especially read "Encouraging Associations" on pages 43–46.

Example 1:

Have listeners think of a teacher from a school they attended previously, one that no one else knows. Ask for the teacher's name and some special characteristics of the teacher. Have other listeners practice association and visualization techniques with the information. At the end of the session, ask the listeners to recall the information.

Example 2:

Have listeners think of the name of a relative who lives far away. Ask other listeners to try to recall the name, place they live, approximate age, and so on using association and visualization strategies. Again ask them to recall the information after a lapse of time. Discuss with them what strategies worked. This activity builds metamemory skills.

Word Lists

Pages 35–37 contain three lists of unrelated words. The words are presented in columns and rows to facilitate the construction of word sets. The majority of the words in the lists were chosen because they are concrete, they represent common objects in the environment, and they are easily visualized or drawn.

The words in *Word List One* are all common objects. In *Word List Two,* the first four columns contain common objects. The fifth column contains abstract nouns (e.g., *east, half*), verbs (e.g., *twist, fight*), and adjectives (e.g., *hot, clean*), which are more difficult to represent. These words are included to provide the option of introducing more difficult material so as to expand the listener's ability to differentiate between the symbol and the word to be recalled. For example, if the word *time* is given, a clock may be used to represent it. In recalling this word, the clock must first be recalled, and then the listener must remember that the clock represents the word *time*. This type of differentiation will be necessary for Sections II, III, and IV, particularly in recall of unusual names. With assistance, the listener will continue to improve this skill.

Word List Three contains some common words (e.g., *trumpet, gate*) and a higher percentage of words that are harder to represent (e.g., *fog, ripple, hero*). It is a more challenging list and should be used only with the most capable listeners.

The words are presented in columns and rows to enable construction of varying lists of unrelated words. Enough words have been provided to accomplish the objective of this section if they are used in the following way: lists can be constructed across the rows, down or up the columns, diagonally, or in various zigzag patterns to provide numerous variations. Figure 5 on page 34 displays a few of the options for choosing words to construct a list.

Figure 5

OPTIONS FOR CONSTRUCTING A LIST

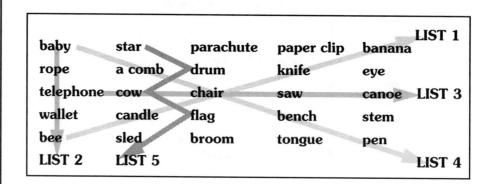

Word List One

a baby*	a star*	a parachute*	paper clip	banana
a rope*	a comb*	a drum*	a knife*	an eye
a telephone*	cow	a chair*	a saw*	a canoe*
wallet	a candle*	a flag*	bench	a stem*
a bee	a sled*	broom	a tongue*	a pen*
a fence*	stove	a hook*	car	a chain*
a needle*	a cage*	a bed*	carrot	a plug*
butterfly	helmet	apple	a hammer*	stairs
a nose*	a duck*	a shoe*	a train*	a cloud*
a skate*	a bubble*	a flower*	a key*	a bottle*
a crown*	a net*	a tree*	a watch*	ear
toothbrush	propeller	a shovel*	balloon	a rat*
a bus*	screwdriver	a snake*	cherry	a card*
leaf	peanut	heart	a bridge*	bell
grape	a book*	bucket	a box*	TV
lightning	fork	a clock*	a swing*	dog
a bowl*	airplane	lips	frog	a finger*
a toe*	squirrel	a nail*	a can*	feather

* An indefinite article is included and should be used in the presentation of this word to avoid ambiguity in meaning.

Word List Two

a flea*	a knee*	shoelace	a glass*	fight
trash	a shell*	a hole*	beggar	electric
skis	the earth	cards	leg	thick
fur	a neck*	penguin	river	clean
triangle	colt	forest	a curl*	east
woman	salt shaker	a plant*	cord	rich
wig	lizard	tennis	calendar	wave
Florida	diamond	wart	the paint	tall
hoof	a stitch*	a wolf*	barber	old
lamp	melon	a belt*	a taxi*	round
beehive	a crab*	violin	uniform	fast
battery	knob	a stamp*	insect	broken
price tag	pillow	a pump*	a circle*	blind
jacket	camera	a claw*	corn	hot
thief	a pocket*	curtain	a record*	twist
a cone*	a stone*	a vacuum*	a crib*	time
turkey	pumpkin	oil can	petal	silver
a spray*	stocking	a tower*	a map*	half

* An indefinite article is included and should be used in the presentation
 of this word to avoid ambiguity in meaning.

Word List Three

a baby*	a star*	a parachute*	paper clip	banana
horseshoe	bug	brain	syrup	cold
robe	rain	butter	paper	grow
tomato	shortstop	inch	web	mile
soap	point	gate	throat	poem
smile	globe	meal	wrench	sweet
trumpet	twig	piano	cork	hero
branch	smoke	curve	janitor	club
letter	valley	tank	cavity	pets
purse	corner	grass	farm	snow
thread	street	money	stick	peel
elbow	blood	drawer	ripple	below
baseball mitt	gallon	eraser	ship	bark
blanket	trail	wire	iron	history
seed	lock	people	cotton	middle
saddle	rug	frame	orchestra	voice
nickel	whale	mountain	label	world
ankle	bleach	run	potato chips	sail
rock	gift	bandage	fog	drill

Summary

The preceding steps in presenting Section I are condensed here. This summary may prove useful in reviewing the steps or may be useful as a guide during presentation.

Step 1: Introducing the Method

Materials

1. The words *dog, tail, mousetrap, chair, man, paint,* and *cat*

Procedure

1. Present the seven words with no assistance for recall.
2. Ask students to repeat them.
3. Tell the association that relates the words.
4. Ask listeners to recall the words.

Step 2: Demonstrating the Method

Materials

1. *Illustrated Cards Sets* (See Appendix E.)

Procedure

1. Present a series of words, one at a time.
2. Present a set of cards demonstrating visualization and association.
3. Emphasize the ridiculous, active associations.
4. Have listeners recall the words from memory.

Step 3: Practicing the Method with Drawings

Materials

1. *Word List One* (See page 35.)
2. Pencils
3. Blank paper

Procedure

1. Slowly present 5 to 10 words from the list.
2. Have participants make associations and create drawings.
3. Encourage imagination, action, and association.
4. Have listeners recall the words from memory.
5. Provide follow-up.

Step 4: Internalizing the Visual Associations

Materials

1. *Word List One* (See page 35.)

Procedure

1. Use no illustrations.
2. Have listeners verbalize their associations.
3. Have listeners recall the words from memory.
4. Provide follow-up.

Step 5: Practicing Independent, Silent Associations

Materials

1. *Word List One* (see page 35), and possibly *Word Lists Two* and *Three* (See pages 36–37.)

Procedure

1. Present the words.
2. Do not have participants verbalize or draw associations.
3. Have participants recall the words from memory.
4. Provide follow-up to improve use of the strategies.
5. Limit the number of sets presented in a session.

Section II

Retention and Recall of Spoken Facts

Goal: The listener will recall facts from a paragraph presented orally.

Rationale

This section involves teaching listeners to associate (1) names, (2) numbers, (3) dates, and (4) places. As stated before, *Listen and Recall* stresses the listener's interaction with auditory information. Association and visual imagery strategies are of primary importance. It is very important to read the explanation of steps given in Section I, especially Steps 2 and 3 on pages 26–29, which discusses association and visual imagery relative to retention and recall. These pages also present important elements that strengthen recall. That discussion is not repeated here or in subsequent sections.

Although Section II can be presented as the first phase in the process of improving a listener's auditory memory, thereby omitting Section I completely, it is preferable to begin with Section I, since it teaches association of words free of context. In Section I, the words are unrelated so they provide a better vehicle for stimulating imaginative associations. For example, if presented with related words such as *dog*, *cat*, and *cow*, one is more likely to depend on semantic categories for memory than if given unrelated words such as *whale*, *tractor*, and *ribbon*. Although using semantic categories is an effective memory strategy, many individuals already use it. By eliminating it as a factor, listeners can focus on learning additional strategies. It is for this reason that unrelated words are a good beginning point for learning the strategies taught with this program.

Materials

The materials for this section are interesting for listeners because they involve unusual facts presented with illustrations. The adult providing intervention shows illustrations to participants to stimulate interest, to encourage visualizing, and to give the context of the oral information to follow.

Appendix F provides 50 *Stimulus Cards*, which should be duplicated onto heavy stock paper and cut out to form cards. Each *Stimulus Card* includes an illustration and a corresponding written paragraph containing facts related to the illustration. The illustration is shown to participants to help orient them to and interest them in the information to be heard. In each paragraph, facts are underlined and the total number of facts is provided to facilitate scoring. General facts are only partially underlined because they represent concepts or ideas rather than specific details. For example, the general idea of "saw the performance" (from *Stimulus Card 39*, "First Circus") could be correctly recalled as "watched the show." However, the location of the first circus, Philadelphia, is a concrete fact and must be recalled exactly.

Appendix G provides outline maps of the United States and the world for use in this section. They may be duplicated. These maps aid in teaching visualization and may be used when presenting the paragraphs on the *Stimulus Cards*.

Presentation

By the time a listener is ready to begin Section II, he or she has gained skill in using strategies for the retention and recall of words. The adult providing intervention then helps in the transition to the next task: retention and recall of spoken facts. This is accomplished by briefly discussing the improvements listeners have made in their listening and memory, the strategies they have learned, and the new ways in which these strategies will be used. Examples of the need for retention and recall of facts may be given (e.g., relating these skills to real life situations) so listeners will understand the usefulness and application of the skills to be gained in this section. If listeners need further encouragement to achieve the goals of Section II, see "Motivating Participants and Monitoring Progress" on pages 16–20.

Orienting the Listeners

Before presenting the stimulus cards, orient listeners to the procedure (i.e., you will be showing them an illustration, reading a paragraph about the illustration, and then asking them to recall facts about the paragraph read). During the presentation of a paragraph, orient listeners to its topic by reading the title on the stimulus card. Show participants the illustration on the card and discuss it briefly.

In addition to the pictorial orientation, verbal orientation is beneficial in the beginning practice sessions. Tell listeners what types of information they should remember. For instance, if the name, place, and date are to be presented, tell them, "You will be asked to recall the name, place, and date." This comment will help to focus listeners' attention. As they become familiar with the task, they will no longer need this type of verbal orientation. They will assume that they are to recall all information presented.

Present the *Stimulus Card* paragraphs and illustrations separately (i.e., first show the illustration is shown to the listeners and then read the paragraph to them without the benefit of seeing the illustration) so that listeners are not visually distracted by the drawings when the facts are presented. Following the orientation to the topic, read the paragraph to the listeners.

Encouraging Associations

Initially, as paragraphs from the stimulus cards are read, discuss possible associations. This keeps listeners actively listening, which facilitates recall. For instance, when a name is presented to participants, they will usually respond with their own associations if given a little encouragement such as, "Do you know anyone with that name? Does it sound like another word to you? Do you hear a word you know in it?" In addition, share your associations as a model for other possibilities. (Several suggestions for associations are given on the following pages. It is important to spend time encouraging a variety of associations so that listeners do not fall into a limited pattern.)

In this way, the associations are taught and practiced. After each stimulus illustration is presented, the paragraph is read, and the associations are made, ask the listeners to recall the facts. Present only two or three cards during one session. Again, as in Section I, listeners asked to recall material presented 5 to 10 minutes before can usually do so, much to their pleasure and surprise.

Gradually, provide less and less help in association and recall. Do this until the listener successfully recalls a high percentage of the facts through the use of his or her own associations. The following sections provide suggestions for encouraging associations.

Names

Several associations may be helpful in remembering names. For example, a friend or relative with the same first or last name can be pictured in the situation described. The initials of the name also are often helpful in aiding retention and recall: *Dan, Raymond,* and *Sue* could be recalled as *D.R.S.*, and *Harvey Kendall* as *H.K.* A third possibility would be recalling a part of the name, such as *Di* for *Diane* or *ar-ar-ar* (laughter) used to recall the name *Arthur*. A fourth possibility, one that was presented in Section I, can be quite entertaining: thinking of ridiculous connections. *Philip* could be pictured *flipping*; *Alexander Haig* could be pictured as *an egg*; *El Salvador* could be remembered as *save a door*.

As an extension activity, it can be fun to take names of famous people in the news and help listeners make strong connections to remember the names. This could be done each week. Each participant in a group could recall a different name and discuss the associations he or she has made. The following week, check the participants' recall by asking, "What was the name you were asked to remember last week?" This may bring a startled, if not panicked, look to their faces, soon to be followed by concentration and a grin of success. Many participants will remember much longer than a week.

Numbers

Ask the listener what meaning a number has as it is presented. Often an association can be made with little encouragement. Connections are often the listener's or a family member's year of birth, someone's age, a birth date, a lucky number, a house number, the number of a sports figure, or a multiple of two numbers (e.g., 18 = 3 x 6).

Heights and weights can be associated with those of the listener or people he or she knows (e.g., 100 pounds is a little less than the listener's weight; 6 feet is about Mark's height; 18 feet is three of Mark standing on top of himself). Associations of large numbers can be made to familiar numbers or estimates of known numbers (e.g., heights of mountains nearby, distances that are known, money that is earned, costs of entertainment centers, costs of cars).

Some listeners will be able to imagine a continuum from 0 to 100 or 0 to 1,000. A place can be estimated and visualized on that line for the number to be recalled. Remembering 48 as just short of halfway to 100 may be effective with some. Seventy-eight would be just a little beyond the three-fourths point. The number 35 will not be recalled as 75 if the listener has pictured one-third of the way along the continuum.

He or she will guess either 35 or a number very close to it. Active involvement with the process of number retention brings the listener nearer the number and usually facilitates more accurate recall.

Dates

Dates may include a month, day, and year. To recall a month, associations may be made with a birthday, with a season (e.g., October—fall; April—spring), or with a holiday (e.g., November—Thanksgiving; July—4th of July). The day or year can be associated with some of the ideas described earlier. In addition, a time line could be developed to recall years. Have participants develop a time line for this century. Have them put the current year on one end and 1900 on the other. Then have them fill in a few dates they know (e.g., birthdays) and ask what other dates they know. Ask if they or family members talk about any wars or the Depression. Other questions might include, "When did cars begin to be used? When was the first airplane flight? When were World Wars I and II?" Encourage listeners to think about or to ask their family members about how they got to school, when they first saw an airplane, and so forth.

Review the time line often and relate dates in the practice materials in Sections II, III, and IV to the time line. Gradually extend the time line back to familiar dates in history. As events in time become more meaningful to the listener, it will be easier for him or her to recall dates. Do not fill the time line up with events. Keep it simple, using the events that are significant for the individual. For example, to recall June 21, 1918, the listener could use a variety of associations. He or she could associate June with the first summer month, warmer weather, and school letting out. Twenty-one is the product of 3 x 7, or counting backwards from 2 to 1, or two-thirds of a month, or an age associated with adulthood. Eighteen could be associated with World War I, the age of most students at high school graduation, or 3 x 6.

Through personal observation, note a particular type of information that is difficult for an individual to recall (e.g., numbers, names). Then adapt the presentation of material to the individual's level (see page 47).

Often the adult providing intervention will discover large gaps in the participants' knowledge of information such as numbers and maps, and these gaps will need to be remediated as part of the process of extending auditory memory. As an example, one participant could not differentiate six inches from six feet. He was taught to know the lengths of his hand and foot and his height, and this helped him to approximate distances more accurately. Many participants can learn to estimate the height of a building (each floor adds about 10 feet to the height), or of posts, grass, books, cars, and so forth.

Places

Places can be associated with a visual image of their approximate location on a map, or with their initials or abbreviations. Places can also be remembered by using the techniques given earlier for recalling names. When a city, state, or country is mentioned, the listener could visualize that place on a map. This will involve visual, spatial, and, in some cases, kinesthetic images. If listeners picture a southern coastal state for an event in Georgia, for example, they will eliminate at least 45 states automatically when asked to recall the location. In addition, the active process of visualizing reinforces the memory.

Use the maps in Appendix G or any map to aid listeners' visualization. The maps also can be helpful in expanding the listeners' knowledge of geography. The purpose is not to teach geography, but to provide orienting schema for memory—that is, some basic knowledge upon which to build. (See "Orienting Schema" beginning on page 15.) A participant's knowledge of the world will grow in meaningful contexts throughout his or her life. References to the map need not be precise for the purpose of memory. A simple outline of a map can be drawn and a quick reference made to it to encourage visualization. A sample dialogue follows:

Adult providing intervention (A): (Show a map of the United States.) Visualize Denver on the map. Point to where it is.

Listener (L): (Points to a spot on the map that approximates the location of Denver.)

A: Okay, visualize that location when you recall the place.

Association can be encouraged also, as illustrated in this dialogue:

A: What do you think of when you think of England?

L: Princess Diana.

A: Okay, visualize Princess Diana in England to help you remember.

Adapting the Presentation for Listeners

The paragraphs on the *Stimulus Cards* do not have to be read verbatim, especially if the number of facts is beyond the listeners' level. Instead, select the facts and the wording appropriate for the listeners. If the information is too lengthy or difficult, simplify it using any of the following methods:

1. Round numbers off. For example, if the information states that a satellite weighs 30.8 pounds, this could be rounded to 31 pounds.

2. Shorten lengthy names and places. For example, Katmandu, Nepal, could be presented simply as Nepal.

3. Omit facts so that there is less to recall. In some cases presentation of a name, location, date, and quantity is challenging enough and provides sufficient practice of the memory strategies.

4. Slow the pace of presentation to allow more time for processing.

5. Repeat information if requested.

6. Provide verbal support for listening and recall memory strategies by encouraging associations as needed. It is important that listeners experience success, because confidence and motivation are critical in learning.

Monitoring Progress

After reading a paragraph from the *Stimulus Cards* (Appendix F), ask listeners to say (or write) the facts from memory. Missing facts can be elicited by asking questions. (Listeners in a small group or large group setting [e.g., a classroom] can respond by writing the facts on paper.) When the intervention is with an individual, answers may be oral. In this section, the emphasis is on recalling the facts. Participants are taught to recall names of people, places, things, numbers, and dates. They are asked questions such as who, what, where, and when, which focus on literal comprehension, rather than why or how questions, which would call for inferential responses. The questions structure the responses and aid in scoring.

How to quantify the recall of facts is detailed below. For example, count each of the following as a fact:

1. A first name
   Example: Ted = 1 fact

2. A last name
   Example: Mozart = 1 fact

3. Each part of a longer name that is unfamiliar to the listener
   Examples: Holly Drive Baptist Church = 4 facts
   Grand Canyon = 1 fact

4. Each month
   Example: July = 1 fact

5. Each day of the week and day of the month
   Example: Tuesday the 10th = 2 facts

6. Each part of a date
   Example: May 18 = 2 facts

7. A city
   Example: Phoenix = 1 fact

8. A state or province
   Examples: Ontario = 1 fact
   Monte Rio, California = 2 facts

9. A country
   Example: Canada = 1 fact

10. Each part of an address
    Example: 23 Windsor Drive = 3 facts

Numbers present more of a problem in quantifying the recall of facts because each number is unique and requires different memory tasks. However, for simplicity when counting facts, the following guidelines are provided:

1. Each number is only one fact.
   Examples: 24,000 = 1 fact
   24 = 1 fact

2. Units of measurement introduce a second fact
   Examples: 24 = 1 fact
   24 feet = 2 facts

Using these guidelines, 2,045 square feet equals two facts (i.e., one for *2,045* and one for *square feet*). The year 1925 is counted as 1 fact.

When scoring, questions may arise concerning unstated, assumed information. Listeners often will omit the parts of an answer that are assumed. This may happen when the question incorporates part of the answer. For example, in the question, "How many people saw the show?" the word *people* is included in the question and, therefore, need not be given in the answer. Omission may also occur when the unit of measurement is obvious. For example, when asked, "How tall is Joe?" the response may be, "five nine." The words *feet* and *inches* may not be spoken, but are assumed. As another example, "89" may be given as an answer to "How hot is it?" The word *degrees* is assumed. Since these answers are not errors of memory, listeners should not be penalized. Therefore, no credit is expected, given, or subtracted for facts that are assumed.

Count the number of facts elicited from participants and record the resulting fraction and percentage of facts recalled (e.g., if 9 out of 15 facts in a paragraph were recalled, the resulting percentage of facts recalled is 60 percent) on a *Progress Sheet* duplicated from Appendix C. When measuring performance toward meeting the objective, the resulting percentage indicates the listener's success.

Also note on the *Progress Sheet* how much help the listener needed. The notation "w/help" (with help) indicates help in thinking of associations was given during the presentation. If no help was given, simply indicate "w/o help" (without help). If only general, nonspecific suggestions were given but none of them were discussed (e.g., "visualize the map"), "some help" could be noted.

The tally for each presentation could be kept separately to clarify how many facts were presented in each set of facts. If three sets are presented in a session, for example, the listener's score might be recorded like this:

Jan. 18—Facts: 6/8 w/help; 4/4 some help; 8/10 w/o help

Since listeners with poor auditory memory may also have auditory discrimination and spelling problems, some leniency is recommended on recall of unfamiliar names. Also, do not penalize for spelling errors when facts are written rather than recited by the listener. This is a listening and memory lesson; spelling concerns would distract from the focus on recall. For further clarification of the system for monitoring progress, examples illustrating how to count facts when partial information is recalled are provided in Appendix H.

Generalization

It would be easy to extend this section by using information from the local newspaper. The following are the texts of newspaper ads and articles describing vehicles for sale, the daily weather report, and employment opportunities. Read an ad or article to listeners and have them apply the visual association strategy to help recall facts. The presentation of two car descriptions or two weather reports, one after the other, should be avoided, because the similarity of the information may cause confusion. Follow up by asking the listeners to think of times this information might be presented orally to them and they would have to recall the details (e.g., hearing the ad on the radio or TV).

Vehicles for Sale

1. 1989 Ford Taurus; 8-cylinder; air conditioning; power windows, locks, steering, and brakes; 60,000 miles; $3295

2. Dodge Ram pickup; 1994; automatic transmission; radio and cassette player; 95,000 miles; $4695

3. Ford Mustang; 1980; 4-cylinder; four-speed; $6600

4. 1929 Model A; 4-door; Town Sedan; 32,000 miles; $7800

5. 1995 GMC truck; 4-wheel drive; black; 39,000 miles; air conditioning; $14,400

Weather Reports

1. Partial hazy sunshine and warm temperatures are in store for today. Highs around 78° F (25° C) cooling to near 73° F (23° C) in the afternoon due to an ocean breeze. Northerly winds will be about 5 to 15 miles per hour by afternoon.

2. Today will be mostly sunny and windy. The high will be around 4° C (39° F). Tonight will become cloudy with lows to -4° C (25° F). Tomorrow will be cloudy with a chance of snow. We may reach a high of 3° C (37° F) tomorrow. The winds will be from the west at 20 to 30 miles per hour.

3. There will be rain in the northwestern states. The rain will become snow over the mountains. There are tornado warnings in the midwestern states. Rain is predicted over the mid-Atlantic states. The only areas of sun will be the southwest and the southern plains.

Employment Opportunities

1. Immediate openings for experienced waiters and waitresses. Apply in person between 4 and 6 p.m. at Rosalita's Restaurant.

2. Secretary needed full time for September in the Roslindale area. Must have excellent word-processing, dictation, and organizational skills. Pleasant phone manner needed. Much client contact.

3. Service station available for sale. Has three bays and office. Fully equipped for good business including wrecker, gas pumps, tools, and equipment.

4. Computer programmer, immediate opening. Second shift, some experience or technical schooling helpful. Call 555-273-3536.

5. Television host for weekly public affairs interview program. Experience necessary. Send resumé and demo tape to: WAND-TV, Box 40, Oldham, NH 55550.

6. Investment firm seeking tax preparer. Capable of completing income tax forms for businesses, individuals, or charities.

7. Senior architect to manage small exhibit design firm involved in zoo and aquarium design. Need 10 years' experience. Knowledge of design and construction methods also required.

8. Drivers wanted to deliver boxes of printed material. Need a good driving record. Must be willing to work hard. Good pay. Excellent benefits.

Section III

Retention and Recall of Information in Spoken Articles

Goal: The listener will recall facts from an article presented orally.

Rationale

By the time the first two sections of *Listen and Recall* have been presented, the strategies of visualizing and creating associations will have become familiar to listeners; however, the strategies will most likely not have become a part of participants' listening outside of the practice situation. The goals of the following two sections of this program are to generalize strategy use to various situations in the listeners' daily lives. Once the listener has practiced applying the strategies to a few articles from Section III, Section IV can be presented as well (see page 13 for an expanded explanation of lesson presentation). For example, one or two articles can be presented in a session along with one oral direction activity. Presenting the lecture-type information in Section III and the oral directions in Section IV promotes generalization because memory strategies are applied to a broad range of situations that simulate real life.

Because the basic listening and memory strategies (i.e., visualization and association) have been explained in the earlier sections, the explanations are not repeated here. However, they remain key strategies in this section. Each lesson in this section also contains additional memory strategies to target as well as suggestions for generalizing use of the strategies.

The adult providing intervention must know the ways to aid recall before using the lessons in this section. Although suggestions for additional memory strategies are included in the lessons, they are not meant to be all-inclusive. Successful use of *Listen and Recall* depends on a thorough knowledge of the strategies described previously and the use of them in a responsive way to develop skills in individual participants. Participants will vary in their willingness, ability, and skills. With strategies in mind, the adult providing intervention uses the lessons merely as "bricks and mortar to build a structure." The explanations of the techniques detailed in the preceding sections are the "architectural plan" to be followed.

Materials

The lessons beginning on page 63 contain articles on a variety of subjects. The syntactic complexity of each is controlled so that participants can concentrate on listening and auditory memory, and not on the comprehension of syntactically complex sentences. In most cases, the sentences contain only one or two clauses. A listing of articles, number of facts, and additional memory strategies targeted in each lesson can be found on page 62.

The articles vary in structure, nature of content, interest level, and level of difficulty. Articles appropriate to a given participant or group of participants should be selected for use; not all articles will be appropriate for all participants. Each lesson includes the reference on which the article is based, ideas for orienting the listeners, memory strategies that might be applied in addition to those previously discussed (i.e., visualization and association), the article information, and suggestions for generalizing memory strategies to real-life situations.

Orienting the Listeners

Before presenting an article, discuss information about the topic to be presented. For instance, the comment, "This is a story about Greek mythology," followed by a brief discussion, can orient the listeners to the topic. In a group setting, a brainstorming session about the topic is a good way to orient the participants. Also, cuing participants by telling them what they are to listen for is helpful.

Additional Memory Strategies

Each lesson provides suggestions for applying additional strategies to aid recall. Visualization and association are viable strategies to apply in this section, but additional strategies also are suggested. The following are the additional strategies suggested and a definition of each:

1. Kinesthetic imagery—imagining or sensing the movement of one's own muscles, tendons, and joints.

2. Rehearsal—repeating information without attaching meaning to it in order to maintain it in working memory.

3. Asking for repetition—asking for the repetition of information after recognizing that the information is important but has been forgotten.

4. Counting—counting the number of items to be remembered; counting is especially useful for lists of information or steps in a sequence.

5. Organization—noticing elements of organization within a presentation such as topics and subtopics or sequential progressions.

6. Knowledge base—activating knowledge about a topic so that new information can be easily processed at a deeper level.

7. Key words—selecting a word or a few words that will easily represent a whole idea.

These suggestions are optional and also can be used in lessons in which they are not presented. For instance, the lesson using the article *Green Berets* suggests using either kinesthetic imagery or the organization of the information as strategies to recall the information. The lesson using the article *Tropical Treetops,* suggests using the organization of the information and key words in the article to help recall the information.

Introduce these strategies at the participants' pace and with their input in selecting the strategies that work best for them. When a participant appears to be proficient in the use of one strategy, another strategy can be introduced. Be aware not to overburden short-term memory. As mentioned earlier, short-term memory has limited capacity. Conscious use of strategies uses space in short-term memory. As strategies become automatic, less short-term memory is used and participants begin to use the strategies subconsciously. The practice provided in the lessons is one way of providing participants with the experience and the opportunity to become strategic learners, which will positively affect their learning experiences.

The Article Information

Each article is presented with important facts underlined; the total number of facts is indicated. The facts include names of people, places, or things; numerical facts; and important concepts. (See Section II, pages 47–49, for a description of how the number of facts is determined.)

Suggestions for Generalization

Each lesson in Section III provides suggestions for generalization to help participants apply memory strategies to real-life situations. The participants should be asked to generate at least one other situation in which each memory strategy could be used in a school situation, the home setting, social activities, or job-related scenarios.

Presentation

Present each lesson by orienting the listeners, then suggesting strategies to aid recall of the facts in the article. Read the article information in a manner simulating classroom lectures or news reports. Since improved auditory memory in daily experience is the goal, presentations should sound conversational rather than read. In addition, the underlining in each article identifies important ideas in much the same way that an outline does; therefore, the facts may be presented in your own words rather than reading the information word for word. Adapt the wording to various localities or cultural groups if necessary.

Recall

After reading the article to the listeners, ask them to tell you as much as they remember. The recalling can also be in written form for groups of participants. If participants are writing their recollections, tell them not to worry about spelling. After listeners have recalled the facts, ask questions to aid their recall of facts if any were missed. Examples of a questioning technique to aid recall are listed in Table 1. In this particular section, one can observe the difference between spontaneous recall and retention. It is interesting to have participants recall facts independently as well as they can and then to observe how many more facts they can recall with questioning or by using other memory strategies.

Table 1

EXAMPLE QUESTIONS

Information Omitted by Participant	Possible Questions
Article: *Early Planes in War*	
1914	Do you remember when this was?
World War I	Do you remember which war?

(Continued)

Table 1—*Continued*

Information Omitted by Participant	Possible Questions
Europe	Where did this happen?
scouting	When planes were first used in war, what did the pilots do? What did they do before they had weapons?
no weapons	Did they carry guns in the beginning?
friendly	How did pilots from enemy countries treat each other?
pistols and rifles	What happened to change the friendliness?
dogfights	What were the fights called?
Snoopy/Peanuts	Do you remember anything about a comic strip? Who is the character in the strip? Which strip was mentioned?
bombs	What else did they have besides rifles and pistols?
pilots/bag of bombs over the side	Who dropped the bombs? How were they carried on the plane? How did the pilot do the bombing?

Article: *Medusa*

three sisters/Gorgons	Who were these creatures? How many were there? How were they related? What were they called?
100 snakes	What did they have on their heads? How many?
poisonous, forked tongue	Tell me about the snakes. What were their tongues like?
fangs	What were the sisters' teeth like?

(Continued)

Table 1—*Continued*

Information Omitted by Participant	*Possible Questions*
brass/claws	What about their hands? What did they look like? What were they made of?
scales	What was on their bodies?
couldn't be cut	How did the scales protect the Gorgons?
wings/shiny gold	What else was on the Gorgons? What were they made of? Describe them.
afraid	How did people react to the Gorgons?
turn to stone	What could the Gorgons do that was terrible?
Medusa	Can you name one Gorgon?
son/Zeus/cutting off her head	There was someone who was supposed to kill Medusa. Do you remember that? Who was it? What was his father's name? How was he going to kill her?

The final step in each lesson is to help participants generalize strategy use to their daily lives. Modify the suggestions for generalization so they are relevant to participants.

Adapting the Presentation

As mentioned previously, not all articles are appropriate for all participants. Some articles may be taxing for participants who have conceptual difficulties or extremely poor memories. The lessons could be adapted for individual participants. This can be accomplished as it was summarized in Section II by doing the following:

1. rounding off numbers;

2. shortening names;

3. omitting certain facts;

4. slowing the pace of the reading;

5. repeating information upon request; or

6. providing verbal support for memory strategies.

The underlines in the articles serve to simplify this task by identifying facts that could be adapted or omitted.

In addition, some articles will not be appropriate to the interests of the participants. Use discretion not only in adapting articles for participants, but also in selecting articles that are appropriate for participants' interests and age levels.

Monitoring Progress

Counting facts recalled provides a way of monitoring progress in participants' responses and provides feedback to participants (and family members, if appropriate). If possible, immediately count facts recalled and give feedback to the participants. Record this data for each session to monitor progress.

As in Section II, each general fact is only partially underlined because in some cases it indicates an idea and not the specific words to be recalled. For example, in the article *Polar Bears, terrible temper* is partially underlined. The listener could verbalize this as "get angry" and receive credit for recalling the idea. The exact words are not important. On the other hand, in the article *Early Planes in War,* the date *1914* is a concrete fact and should be recalled exactly. Numbers and common names require accuracy. By this time, listeners have gained experience and skill in retention and recall of facts. They are expected to recall numbers and common names with accuracy. However, in this section, be lenient for recall of unusual names.

Correct recall of a fact is sometimes implied in the way a participant tells or writes the data, rather than being stated directly. For instance, in recalling the article *Early Planes in War,* the listener may say that "Pilots began shooting at each other" rather than saying that they started using pistols and rifles. Or in recalling the article *May Pierstorff,* the listener may say that "it is only legal to mail baby chicks," which implies that it was illegal to mail live animals but it was not illegal to mail baby chicks, which is the way the article originally presented the information.

Listeners express ideas in a variety of ways. Decide when to judge the ideas for content and not for the exact wording given to them. The same distinction can be made in classroom situations. Some information is purely factual and is likely to be on classroom exams. Similarly, in a work environment, some information must be memorized verbatim (e.g., exactly how to answer the telephone if you are a receptionist), while other information may be recalled in general terms (e.g., how to close the office at the end of the day).

Two important categories of information can be maintained to monitor participants' progress. The first type of monitoring requires recording the number of facts recalled for each article (e.g., noting that a participant recalled 10 of 12 facts). The second type of monitoring is to keep a record of the strategies used and how effectively the participant used them.

Numerical Data

To monitor progress by counting, count the facts recalled and record the number of facts recalled over the number of facts presented to form a fraction (i.e., 7/13 facts recalled). These data then easily convert to a percentage (in this case, 54 percent). The title of the article, the date, the number of items recalled over the facts presented, and the resulting percentage can be recorded on a *Progress Sheet* (Appendix C; see Figure 2, page 17, for an example of a completed *Progress Sheet)*. To monitor improvement over time, calculate the percentage of facts recalled from several lessons (rather than individually for each lesson) over several weeks to observe trends.

When counting facts, count those facts recalled spontaneously and those recalled in response to questions. This is done for two reasons: First, this reflects the fact that questions are often a part of the educational process (e.g., class participation, tests) and are often part of social and business interactions. In other words, recall often functions in interactive situations rather than in isolation. Second, the assumption is made that if a participant can answer the questions accurately, the information has been retained in his or her memory. If desired, record the number of facts recalled independently versus the number of facts recalled through questioning.

When reporting progress to participants, be specific about their skills and improved performance rather than just reporting numbers. Discuss qualitative observations regarding the use of memory strategies as well.

Recording Strategy Use

It will be helpful to participants to become consciously aware of the strategies available to them and to try them out. Although the use of strategies eventually will become automatic and possibly unconscious, an initial awareness of what they are, and where and when to apply them, empowers participants to use them in other situations. Strategy use can be recorded on the same *Progress Sheet* used for recording numerical data, or a separate *Progress Sheet* can be maintained. Either way, track use of memory strategies along with participants' comments related to effectiveness of their strategy use in different situations.

As strategies are practiced, participants will begin to choose the ones with which they are comfortable and will adapt them to fit their styles. This usually occurs without additional assistance. The first two sections of *Listen and Recall* emphasized two strategies: association and visualization. Section III (and also Section IV) provides the opportunity to practice those strategies as well as additional memory strategies. Participants will become more independent and recall information more easily and quickly.

Factors Affecting Performance

Syntax and vocabulary are fairly well controlled in the articles. Sentences are kept short, rarely exceeding two clauses, and vocabulary is rarely beyond a sixth-grade level. Other factors affecting successful recall include the familiarity of the content, listener interest in the content, and concept difficulty. Of course, an always-present factor in performance is motivation. For these reasons, performance will not necessarily improve steadily, but rather anecdotal notes over a period of time will yield the most helpful information about a generalized trend of progress. As with Section II, note the amount of support needed by the listener to associate, visualize, and use other memory strategies during the recall task.

Section III Lessons

Page #	Title	No. of Facts	Additional Memory Strategies
63	*Early Planes in War*	14	kinesthetic imagery
64	*May Pierstorff*	19	rehearsal; asking for repetition
66	*Iroquois Indians*	14	rehearsal; asking for repetition
67	*Ballerina Coach*	10	kinesthetic imagery
68	*Polar Bears*	15	organization
70	*Diamonds*	14	knowledge base
72	*Medusa*	21	kinesthetic imagery; organization
74	*Green Berets*	18	counting; kinesthetic imagery; organization
76	*Fire under a Town*	27	kinesthetic imagery
77	*Black Turtles*	30	organization; key words
79	*News Reporter*	17	knowledge base
81	*Columbia*	26	key words
83	*Trapped in Snow*	23	counting; asking for repetition; kinesthetic imagery
85	*The Hubble Telescope*	42	organization; key words
87	*Creation of the World...*	45	organization; knowledge base
89	*Tropical Treetops*	41	key words; organization
91	*Exploring a River*	60	knowledge base
94	*Dinosaurs*	15	counting; key words
96	*Iceman*	37	key words
98	*California*	53	knowledge base

Early Planes in War

Reference: Air Force, United States (1962). In *The World Book encyclopedia* (Vol. 1, pp. 155–156). Chicago: Field Enterprises.

Orienting the Listener

The first plane was flown in 1903. Early planes stayed up for only a few minutes and didn't go very far or very high. This information will tell you about planes in World War I. (Discuss the dates to expand listener knowledge about time.) Planes had not been flown very long before World War I. They had never been used in a war before.

Additional Memory Strategy: Kinesthetic Imagery

You have some excellent strategies for remembering names and dates. Some people use their bodies to help them recall as well. In this article it may help if you imagine that you are a pilot. You may be able to feel yourself flying the plane, looking out the window, and using the items that I mention. You could imagine you are doing these things.

The Information (14 Facts)

The first airplanes used in war were used in World War I. World War I began in 1914 in Europe. At first, the planes were used to scout the enemy to see where they were. They didn't have weapons on the planes then. Pilots of enemy countries were friendly to each other and would wave to each other as they flew by.

Soon pilots started using pistols and rifles. The friendliness stopped as they began shooting at each other. The fights between pilots were known as dogfights. You'll often see Snoopy in the comic strip "Peanuts" pretending to be one of these pilots.

Another weapon was added to airplanes: bombs. The first bombs were dropped from planes by the pilots. A pilot would keep a bag of bombs beside him. When he wanted to bomb something, he would reach into the bag. He would drop a bomb over the side of the airplane.

Suggestions for Generalization

Pretend you need to remember the names, jobs, and locations of several people at your new job. For example, Donna Pierce is an accountant on fourth floor; Carmella Liggins is an engineer on first floor; Charles Ritsema is a copy editor on fifth floor. How could you recall these facts?

May Pierstorff

Reference: Wallace, I., Wallechnisky, D., and Wallace, A. (1982, January 10). Significa: The parcel post kid. *Parade Magazine*, p. 20.

Orienting the Listener

This is a really unusual story. It's true. It's about a little girl who was mailed to her grandmother. You will need to remember many facts, such as names, places, and numbers, so use all of your strategies to remember.

Additional Memory Strategies: Rehearsal; Asking for Repetition

If a name is unusual or unfamiliar to you, it can seem very difficult to remember. It helps to say the name correctly several times (rehearsal). You can ask me to repeat it just like you can ask a teacher to repeat in class or a supervisor to repeat at work. You may want to figure out how many syllables are in a word and to make sure that you get all of the syllables. If you can say it, you are more likely to recall it. For example, in remembering the term *homeostasis*, you would be sure that you could pronounce it correctly. A science book could help you either in one of its chapters or in the glossary. You could also use a dictionary. You would look for the number of syllables and make sure that you could say each one and then put the syllables together.

The Information (19 Facts)

The girl's name was <u>May</u> <u>Pierstorff.</u> (Ask the listener, "What connections can you make with that name?") Her parents wanted to send her to visit her <u>grandmother</u>, but <u>train tickets</u> were too expensive. She needed to travel from <u>Grangeville</u>,* Idaho, to <u>Lewiston</u>, <u>Idaho</u>, which was <u>100</u> <u>miles</u> away. (Pause and say to the listener, "Picture Idaho on the map.") The year was <u>1914</u>. May was <u>4 years</u> old. She weighed 48 pounds. (Say, "I've told you many facts. Let me make some connections. Do you know anyone 14 years old? That could help you remember the date.") The parents decided to mail May. They took her to the post office. Nothing could be mailed that weighed over <u>50</u> pounds. May was just <u>48</u> <u>pounds</u>. Also, it was <u>illegal to mail live</u> animals, but it was <u>not illegal to mail baby chicks</u>. So May was called a baby chick. Her parents bought <u>53</u> <u>cents</u> worth of stamps. The stamps were put on a <u>card</u> <u>tie</u>d to her coat. Away she went in the <u>baggage car</u>.

*Omit some of the geographical names if this is too difficult.

Suggestions for Generalization

If you make a absurd association to help you remember a word, your association will be slightly different from the original word. You remember the silly association to remind you of the real word. For instance, for a science class you could remember the term *mitosis* by thinking of "my toe's sis." To remember the city name *Merrimack*, you could imagine a "merry Big Mac." It could be a big burger with a smile on its face. When you need to recall the word, you will first think of the absurd association and then the real word.

For example, imagine that you have to memorize the parts of the cell for biology class. Your test will include a picture of the cell and you have to list the name and function of each part. Three facts need to be connected for each cell part—the shape, the name, and the function. A *ribosome*, for instance, is the name of the part of the cell in which proteins are made. Ribosomes look like dots attached to a bent line. I will make a silly association between the key words just as we have been practicing. I'm going to take the word "rib" out of *ribosome* and imagine that it is a barbequed rib with meat on it. Since meat is a protein, that is my connection with the function. I will imagine that when I look at the ends of the bones, they look like dots. I now have a silly story that connects the three pieces of information. You may not remember them, but I will remember them because I thought of them. If I do the thinking, I will remember it. If you do the thinking, you will remember it. Now it's your turn. Connect these: golgi bodies (name) that store and release chemicals (function) and look like a fat "i" (shape).

Describe another situation where you could apply this strategy.

Iroquois Indians

References: Bragdon, H., and McCutchen, S. (1978). *History of a free people*. New York: Macmillan.

O'Connor, J.R. (1978). *Exploring American history*. Englewood Cliffs, NJ: Globe Books.

Orienting the Listener

Some people believe that the United States Constitution came, in part, from ideas from the Iroquois federation. Listen, and I think you may hear some similarities.

Additional Memory Strategies: Rehearsal; Asking for Repetition

(This discussion assumes that the article *May Pierstorff* was previously used as a listening activity.) Remember when we read the story about the little girl who was mailed to her grandmother? We talked about remembering difficult names. This article has some difficult names also. What are some ways of dealing with them? (See page 64 for a reminder.)

The Information (14 Facts)

Several Native American tribes lived in the area that is now the state of N<u>ew York</u>. These tribes fought with each other. Two chiefs decided to end this fighting. Their names were <u>Dekanawida</u> and <u>Hiawatha</u>. Under the leadership of these two chiefs, <u>five</u> <u>tribes</u> joined together to form the <u>Iroquois League</u>. This probably happened in the <u>1500s.</u>

The Iroquois League was run by a council of <u>50</u> <u>chiefs</u>. In each of the five tribes, <u>women</u> c<u>hose chief</u>s to represent them at the League council. If the women of a tribe didn't think a chief was doing a good job, they c<u>hose a different</u> chief.

The 50 chiefs settled arguments <u>between</u> tribes and helped them live peacefully with one another. Each tribe, however, <u>ruled itself</u> and remained independent.

Suggestions for Generalization

In social studies class, or when reading a newspaper article or listening to the news, you often need to remember difficult names. Pick a difficult name and let's discuss how you can use visual association to remember the name.

Ballerina Coach

Reference: Micheli, L.J. (1980). *Sports medicine*. Presentation to parents' group, Newton, MA.

Orienting the Listener

This is a true story about football practice.

Additional Memory Strategy: Kinesthetic Imagery

In this article, when you hear references to injuries, stretching exercises, warm-ups, and the ballerina coach, you might imagine yourself moving or you might visualize the actions. (By using the word *imagine*, you allow the participants to use the skills that come naturally to them. Some participants will more readily visualize this article, and others will imagine themselves moving.)

The Information (10 Facts)

Until the 1970s, many professional football players were injured in the preseason practice sessions and games. A new coach for the Pittsburgh Steelers began doing something unusual to prevent injuries. He began using slow, stretching exercises to warm up his team. People had never heard of this in profootball and found it very funny. They called him "the ballerina coach." They teased the coach and the team about their warm-ups.

During the first season of stretching exercises, the Steelers had fewer than half as many injuries as other teams. Other teams began to use the same exercises. They did not want to have their good players sidelined with injuries.

Suggestions for Generalization

Tell me the name of your favorite team, player, position, and player number. I'll try to remember them using memory strategies. (This is an opportunity to model memory strategies in a situation similar to one that participants may experience. You could ask for this information before reading the article and then retell the information after the article has been read and facts recalled. If you forget or make a mistake, you can model two things: recognition that we all make mistakes and it's okay to do so, and metamemory skills of examining what worked and what didn't and how you could have done better. To further extend this into the participant's life, ask if there is any particular sports information he or she would like to recall. If the participant is knowledgeable about sports, this knowledge base may make it very easy for him or her to recall.)

Polar Bears

Reference: National Public Radio. (1981, October 6). *News presenta-tion*. Boston: WBUR.

Orienting the Listener

This may seem like a strange question, but do you know what color a polar bear is? (Allow for a brief discussion.) Now I'll let you know why it was important to talk about the color of polar bears.

Additional Memory Strategy: Organization

The organization of this article is somewhat complex. There is a problem, an attempt to solve it, a minor problem, a solution to the minor problem, a finding, and then a solution to the original problem.

The Information (15 Facts)

This is about a problem at zoos. The p<u>olar bear</u>s were <u>turning gree</u>n. People started complaining. They wanted to see white polar bears.

A zoo hired a <u>biologist</u> to find out why the bears were green. He asked the zoo to s<u>end him a strand of gree</u>n fur from a bear.

That was a problem. How do you get fur from such a dangerous animal? Polar bears have t<u>errible temper</u>s and <u>long, sharp claw</u>s.

The zookeepers invented a fur snatcher. It was a piece of a <u>saw</u> on a <u>long pole</u>. A zookeeper pulled the saw across a bear's thick fur coat and got some fur.

When the biologist looked at the fur, he found tiny green <u>plants</u> growing o<u>n each stran</u>d. The plants are called <u>algae</u>. The algae didn't hurt the bear.

The zookeepers knew what the problem was. They needed a solution to the problem. The solution was actually very simple. The bears had pools to swim in. The pools were filled with freshwater. The algae were freshwater algae. That means the algae grew only in freshwater, like lake water. The algae c<u>ouldn't stand sal</u>t in their water. P<u>olar bears are use</u>d to salt. There is salt in the ocean where the polar bears come from. So the problem was solved. <u>Salt</u> was added to the <u>pools</u> at the zoo. There were no more green polar bears.

Suggestions for Generalization

Let's say you are going on a vacation. A friend tells you about a great restaurant to visit on your vacation. (Have a participant tell you the name of a unique restaurant.) How will you remember the name "_____"?

Diamonds

Reference: Conkey, S. (1981, March 29). It's finders keepers in this diamond field. *The Boston Globe* [Travel section], p. 47.

Orienting the Listener

This is about an unusual place in the United States where you can go camping.

Additional Memory Strategy: Knowledge Base

(As participants progress in their listening skills, you want them to remember more meaningful associations. You want them to recall not only a number, but what that number represents. Numbers can be challenging, particularly for younger adolescents, because they have fewer associations with them. For example, their knowledge of dates in history is often limited, and their experience with money is limited as well. As part of the process of building listening skills, it is helpful to build knowledge so that associations are more meaningful.)

In this article there are four numbers, each of which is related to the story in a meaningful way. For example, 500 is more than a number, it is the number of diamonds found. One hundred thousand represents the number of dollars a few diamonds are worth. The two dates in the article are related to specific events. To recall the facts, it will be helpful to attach meaning to these isolated facts. Large sums of money may become meaningful to you when you relate them to salaries of bus drivers, accountants, pilots, soldiers, or sports figures. The cost of new or used cars can help you give meaning to sums of money. Dates can be meaningful if you connect them to other time lines, important events in time, or birthdays of persons you know.

The Information (14 Facts)

You have a chance to find your own diamond. Just take a camping trip to Crater of Diamonds State Park in Arkansas. You are allowed to dig for diamonds and keep what you find. More than 500 diamonds a year are found. A few of them are worth more than $100,000 (one hundred thousand dollars).

The area was first discovered to be rich in diamonds in 1906. It is the only place in North America where diamonds are found naturally.

The state of Arkansas bought the diamond fields in <u>1972</u>. Before that, there were many shady adventures there in which people <u>lied, cheated and stole</u>.

Suggestions for Generalization

There are some wonderful national parks. Each is very different. Let's say you keep getting the names of the parks mixed up. You want to think of a way to remember that Yellowstone is in Wyoming and has geysers, and Yosemite is in California and has waterfalls. How can you use memory strategies to keep that straight?

Medusa

Reference: Hawthorne, N. (1955). The Gorgon's head. In H.W. Mabie (Ed.), *Myths every child should know* (pp. 51–80). Garden City, NY: Houghton Mifflin.

Orienting the Participant

This is a story from Greek mythology. Myths are stories that ancient people told to answer their questions about the world around them.

Additional Memory Strategies: Kinesthetic Imagery; Organization

When listening to this article, you could use your body, in addition to using other techniques, to help you remember the information. I will be describing a monster. You can imagine that you are that monster. As I describe a part of the monster's body, imagine how it would feel if your body was like that.

In addition to using the kinesthetic imagery strategy, you could use an organization strategy. Let's briefly go over the article's organization. (Head, hands, body; then danger or fear; then killing her.)

The Information (21 Facts)

There were <u>three</u> <u>sisters</u>. They were ugly monsters called <u>Gorgons</u>. They had <u>100</u> wriggling <u>snakes</u> instead of hair on their <u>heads</u>. Each snake had a <u>poisonous, forked tongue</u>. Each sister had long <u>fangs</u> for teeth.

The sisters' hands were long, <u>brass claw</u>s. Their <u>bodies</u> were covered with <u>scales</u> that <u>couldn't be cut</u>. They had <u>wings</u> and could fly. Every feather in their wings was made of beautiful, <u>shiny gold</u>.

When the sisters flew about, the people hid from them. They were <u>afraid</u> of them. They were afraid of the Gorgons' sharp fangs, their claws, and the poisonous snakes. But even worse than that, if any person <u>looked into the face</u> of a Gorgon, the person would immediately <u>turn to stone</u> forever.

You may have heard of one of these sisters, <u>Medusa</u>. She was one of the Gorgons. The <u>son</u> of the god <u>Zeus</u> was given the job of <u>cutting off her head</u>.

Suggestions for Generalization

Pretend you are asked to bring some baseball equipment to the game on Saturday. You need to remember to bring three balls, the bases, five bats, and your uniform. How can you remember what you need to bring?

Green Berets

Reference: Moore, R. (1981, August 2). The green berets are back. *Parade Magazine*, (pp. 6–8).

Orienting the Listener

This is about a part of the United States Army called the Green Berets. Have you heard of them? They are specially trained.

Additional Memory Strategies: Counting; Kinesthetic Imagery; Organization

When someone says he or she is going to tell you five things or two things or several things, it alerts you to listen for a list. For example, if someone invites you to a party and says you need to bring a few things, you know you have to listen for a list. In this article, you will hear me say that there are several skills Green Berets learn. You will definitely want to use visual imagery to recall the skills, but you can also try counting them so that when you try to recall them you will know when you have finished your list. It is a good aid to helping you remember.

A kinesthetic imagery strategy may be also helpful in remembering the facts in the information I'm going to tell you. I will give hints about how to do this as we go along. Also, as you are listening, picture your body acting out what you hear.

(Discuss this third strategy after presenting the information.) Sometimes you can use the organization of the article to help you remember. I'll take you through the organization. See if it could have helped you remember anything new.

First I told you how the Green Berets are different: I told you about their groups, the attacks, and the pain.

Then I told you about the special skills they learn. You could have pictured yourself doing several things. Try to remember your gestures.

Then I talked about exercising.

The Information (18 Facts)

The <u>army</u> has a special team of soldiers called the <u>Green Beret</u>s. Because they are trained to fight in <u>small group</u>s, they can pester the enemy with <u>surprise attack</u>s. They are taught to be tough and to fight even when they are injured and <u>in pain</u>. (Pause and say to the listener, "Picture your body reacting to an injury.")

Green Berets learn several important skills. Each one learns to be an expert <u>parachutist</u>. He also learns to <u>survive alone</u> in the wilderness for days without carrying food or water. He has to find his own food. He learns to <u>avoid being captured</u>. He learns how to <u>train others</u> to be soldiers. He learns about <u>weapons</u>, <u>explosives</u>, and <u>communications</u>. (Say, "Picture yourself doing these things." Encourage and/or model associated body gestures.)

(As you present this paragraph, pause several times in the reading to encourage body reactions.) Green Berets are physically very strong. Each <u>morning</u> they <u>run two or more</u> <u>miles</u> with <u>40</u> <u>pound packs</u> on their backs. They do it again in the <u>evening</u>. They also do other exercises. All of their specialized training makes them a team of expert fighters.

Suggestions for Generalization

Before going to visit a friend, you have to do four things: mow the lawn, clean the bathroom, brush the cat, and call your grandmother. How could you use counting, visualization, or absurd associations to remember the four tasks?

Fire under a Town

Reference: Siegel, B. (1981, March 29). For 19 years, fire rages under town. From *The Los Angeles Times* in *The Boston Globe*, p. 46.

Orienting the Listener

This is about a fire that has burned for a long time.

Additional Memory Strategy: Kinesthetic Imagery

As you listen to this story, it may sound like a news report. Imagine the reporter showing you these events "at the scene." Imagine being at the fire.

The Information (27 Facts)

In <u>May</u> of <u>1962</u>, a fire started in a town <u>dump</u> in <u>Pennsylvania</u>. The fire spread to a <u>coal mine</u> and burned for more than <u>18 years</u>. People <u>tried many ways</u> to put it out, but nobody had been able to do it. It was hard to get enough money to put the fire out. The best way of putting out the fire was too expensive. The cheaper ways did not work. The fire spread to <u>140 acres</u> and was burning <u>under the home</u>s of many families in the town of <u>Centralia</u>.

Dangerous and deadly <u>gases</u> were entering the <u>basements</u> of some homes. One basement heated up to <u>180 degrees</u>. A <u>12-year-old</u> boy named <u>Todd</u> was standing in his <u>grandmother's backyard</u> when the ground <u>caved in</u>. He began to fall into the mine fire. He grabbed <u>tree roots</u> and was pulled out of the hole by his <u>cousin, Eric</u>.

Over <u>three million</u> <u>dollars</u> were spent in <u>seven</u> <u>tries</u> to stop the fire.

Suggestions for Generalization

Tape-record or videotape a current news report from the radio or TV. Have participants practice using memory strategies using this recording. If the pace is too fast, slow it down by using the recorder's pause button.

Black Turtles

Reference: Wexler, M. (1981, June-July). Yankee don't go home. *National Wildlife, 19*(4), 4–11.

Orienting the Listener

You probably have heard about salmon returning home to lay eggs. They swim back from the ocean to the stream where they were born. This is about another animal that does this.

Additional Memory Strategies: Organization; Key Words

This article progresses from one topic to another. Let's listen for these topic changes and find key words that will help you recall the ideas in each section.

The Information (30 Facts)

The place is a beach in Mexico. Black turtles have returned to the beach where they were born. Some of these amazing turtles swam 1000 miles to return home. Since they weigh 100 pounds, it is hard for them to struggle up onto the beach. You can hear their heavy breathing. In the ocean they are graceful swimmers, but it is hard for them to move on land.

They have returned to lay their eggs. They struggle up the beach and dig a hole for the eggs. Each turtle lays about 100 eggs. It takes three hours for them to lay the eggs. Each egg is about the size of a tennis ball.

A few years ago, people were killing the turtles while they were on the beach. Remember, they are slow so they are easy to kill. So many were killed over the years that they were in danger of becoming extinct. People sold the turtle meat for food. The shells were used for making jewelry. The hide, the skin, was used like leather for boots and bags. The turtle oil was used for making cosmetics. People also paid much money for the eggs. Many big turtles were killed, and many eggs were stolen.

Those were not the only problems for the turtles. When they are just hatched, the baby turtles hurry off to the ocean. Many animals that enjoy eating baby turtles. The babies are in great danger. Crabs and dogs are two of the many animals that eat turtle babies.

Kim Cliffton wanted to do research on the turtles. He discovered they were being killed. He risked his life to save the turtles. People threatened him. Someone shot holes into his house. But these great turtles are now protected. Only a certain number can be killed. Hopefully, now the black turtles will survive and reproduce.

Suggestions for Generalization

Let's pick some key words from your book (this could be, for example, a textbook or a technical manual for operating an appliance) and practice memorizing the key words and their meanings. We'll follow these steps for each key word: (1) Practice the word until you pronounce it correctly. (2) Look for the meaning and make sure you understand it. It is difficult to recall what we do not understand. (3) Find a way to associate the word with the meaning.

News Reporter

References: Krause, C. (1980, June 12). This would be no way to end your career. From *The Washington Post* in *The Boston Globe* [U.S. and world section], p. 3.

Kinzer, S. (1980, June 12). She's fighting for Argentina. *The Boston Globe* [U.S. and world section], p. 3.

Orienting the Listener

This is a true story. It happened in South America just a few decades ago. This story helps me to appreciate the Bill of Rights that protects our rights in this country. In the article, I will refer to an embassy.

Additional Memory Strategy: Knowledge Base

(Some listeners will not know what an embassy is. To improve their knowledge base and therefore make recall easier, discuss this concept with them.) Knowing what an embassy and the Bill of Rights are will help you recall information in this article. Let's talk about these terms.

The Information (17 Facts)

An American news reporter was covering a story in Bolivia in 1980. He was staying in a hotel. He was taken out of his hotel by five army intelligence agents. While he was still in his hotel lobby, he thought quickly. He had to let the United States embassy know that he was being taken so that they could protect him. Otherwise, he might be held by the government and no one would know. A hotel receptionist quickly dialed the embassy for him. He told them where he was going.

Some countries have a bill of rights to protect the people's rights. But in many countries, people don't have such rights. Luckily for this reporter, the United States has a Bill of Rights. The United States embassy checked on him and he was released after two and one-half hours of questioning.

In another country in South America, Argentina, the right to life and liberty has been severely violated. At least 15,000 people have disappeared, according to Amnesty International. Amnesty International is an organization that is based in London. It is concerned about human rights. Other groups investigating human rights in Argentina claim that there is persecution there. The government has denied it.

Suggestions for Generalization

Let's look at a recent magazine and find a name or term that is challenging to remember. (Other ideas, in addition to the comet Hyakutake, are the names of political candidates, performers, or new terms.) What are some strategies you can use to help you recall the name or term?

Columbia

Reference: Cooke, R. (1981, April 15). Perfect landing caps Columbia's first trip. *The Boston Globe*, pp. 1, 10.

Orienting the Listener

This is about the space shuttle Columbia.

Additional Memory Strategy: Key Words

As you are listening and remembering information, we will pick out key words that will help you recall the information. (Examples of key words include first bunch [paragraph 1], reused [paragraph 2], slow down [paragraph 3], heat [paragraph 4], and landing [paragraph 5].)

The Information (26 Facts)

The space shuttle Columbia was another important step into space. Columbia was first launched on April 12, 1981. It landed back on Earth almost three days later.

How was Columbia different? It was the first spacecraft that could be used again. Earlier spacecraft either kept traveling in space and did not return, or they were not able to be reused.

Astronauts John Young and Robert Crippen piloted the first space shuttle. They orbited the Earth 36 times. To come back to Earth, they had to turn Columbia around. Then they fired the shuttle's small maneuvering rockets. This slowed Columbia down so that it could leave its orbit and re-enter the atmosphere. When Columbia re-entered the atmosphere, there was a lot of friction. The friction caused the shuttle to heat up. Scientists expected Columbia to heat up to 2,700 degrees Fahrenheit. It was covered with special tiles to protect it from the heat.

Columbia landed in the Mojave Desert. It landed as a glider is landed—without power. The landing was perfect. The astronauts were excited. Astronaut Young said, "We're really not too far from going to the stars. Bob and I might try it sometime."

Suggestions for Generalization

(Give each participant a pretend name that only he or she will know.) You each have an alias name. We will practice introducing ourselves to others in the group. The goal is to remember everyone's new name for the entire session. Think of associations you can use to remember the alias names. Remember that the more ridiculous they are and the more active your visualization is, the easier it will be to recall the names. (Discuss where else participants would find themselves in a similar situation [e.g., a party, a business gathering, a new class].)

Trapped in Snow

Orienting the Listener

Additional Memory Strategies: Counting; Asking for Repetition; Kinesthetic Imagery

The title of this article is *Trapped in Snow*. The title gives you a strong indication of what this article will be about.

This article will list several things the people had to carry with them. It is a list of things you can count. You may be able to tell that the list is coming when you hear the tone of my voice. Often when people list things, they use a different tone of voice. Listen to me listing some things I need for a class I'm taking: I need four notebooks, a pencil, and a calculator. How many things did I say? You can use counting as one strategy for remembering. (Discuss the tone of voice and the rhythm.) Here's another list of things to take skiing: I need to remember my ski boots, a wool hat, my skiis, my poles, my jacket, and some money. How many things did I list?

Were you also able to visualize the ski equipment to recall the items? Did you picture them or use your body? Right near the beginning of this article, I will tell you a list. Count the things in my list, but also visualize using them to help you recall. If you want me to repeat them, you can ask. Asking speakers to repeat is a great strategy.

Counting is an important memory strategy, because it allows you to know when you are missing information and helps you to know when you have remembered everything. For example, when you recall the Great Lakes, you stop thinking of them when you have remembered five. You know there are only five of them, so you stop then.

(If a listener uses a kinesthetic imagery strategy, he or she might imagine the feeling of the ski clothing or imagine getting ready to ski, putting socks, boots, and a jacket on, and so forth. A visual person may imagine this entirely differently by "seeing" the skis, books, hat, poles, jacket, and money.)

The Information (23 Facts)

Three men were out skiing for four days. They carried all of their supplies on their backs: food, clothes, tent, maps, and sleeping bags. Each night when they set up camp, they figured out exactly where they were on the map. On their third night, they camped on a ridge. On two sides of them, there were cliffs. The next day, they planned to ski down the ridge. In the morning, they looked out to find a "whiteout." That means that the snow made it impossible for them to see very far. They could barely see their own hands if they held their arms out straight. Any travel that day would be dangerous. They could fall off a cliff if they couldn't see the edge. They a<u>te breakfast</u> in the tent. After breakfast, they took out their maps. With their <u>compasses</u> and <u>map</u>, they figured out exactly what angle they must travel. They t<u>ied themselves togethe</u>r with a long rope that allowed them to stay connected. If one fell over a cliff, the others would c<u>atch hi</u>m with the rope. On<u>e of the</u>m would ski ahead at the correct c<u>ompass angl</u>e. He w<u>ould sto</u>p and wait for the others to follow the rope. In this way, they slowly worked their way down from the ridge.

Suggestions for Generalization

How else could you apply a kinesthetic strategy to remembering the facts in this article (e.g., imagining the weight of the supplies on their backs, the fear of being lost or falling off the ridge, and the feeling of a whiteout)? What are other situations in which remembering could improve if you used a kinesthetic strategy (e.g., to remember grocery items for a meal, imagine assembling ingredients and cooking them; to remember items to pack for a camping trip, imagine each activity you might do on the camping trip)?

The Hubble Telescope

References: Naeye, R. (1996, August). Hubble's birthday bash. *Astronomy*, *24*(8) 30–35.

Wilford, J.N. (1993, December 11). Shuttle releases Hubble telescope. *The New York Times* [National report], 11.

Orienting the Listener

Let's talk about what an astronaut is and what an astronomer is. They are very similar words. How are the words alike? Who knows what an astronaut is? Who knows what an astronomer is? Do you know any other words that are related like these two are? In this story, I will talk about both astronomers and astronauts.

Additional Memory Strategies: Organization; Key Words

The first paragraph, or introductory comments, usually gives general information so you will know the topic. Then it gets more specific. Notice the changes in ideas as you listen. What changes can you notice? (Note: If you are discussing the organization after the article is presented and recalled, you can use the listeners' notes to identify ideas and key words. Examples of key words could include: paragraph 2—*shimmer* or *atmosphere*; paragraph 3—*problem* or *lens*; paragraph 4—*repair* or *space walks*; and paragraph 5—*discoveries*.)

The Information (42 Facts)

Amazing new discoveries are being made by astronomers. One reason is the Hubble space telescope. The Hubble was launched in April of 1990. It is about the size of a bus. It is orbiting the earth.

Because the Hubble is orbiting above our atmosphere, it takes better pictures than a telescope on Earth. The atmosphere shimmers and makes stars twinkle. The Hubble orbits above the shimmering, and so it gets a better picture.

A few weeks after it was launched, some problems were discovered. Part of the telescope's lens was ground incorrectly. The error was so tiny that it was only one-fiftieth of the width of a human hair. But, because of that small error, the telescope gave scientists blurry pictures.

In December of 1993, seven astronauts went up in the space shuttle Endeavor to repair the Hubble. They went on space walks on five different da̲y̲s. The repairs worked, and a̲stronomers are l̲e̲a̲r̲n̲i̲n̲g̲ ̲m̲a̲n̲y̲ ̲n̲e̲w̲ t̲h̲i̲n̲g̲s̲ ̲a̲b̲o̲u̲t̲ ̲t̲h̲e̲ ̲u̲n̲i̲v̲e̲r̲s̲e̲.

A d̲o̲t̲ ̲o̲f̲ ̲l̲i̲g̲h̲t̲ that looks like a t̲i̲n̲y̲ ̲s̲t̲a̲r̲ in a t̲e̲l̲e̲s̲c̲o̲p̲e̲ ̲o̲n̲ ̲E̲a̲r̲t̲h̲ may be really a cluster of t̲h̲o̲u̲s̲a̲n̲d̲s̲ ̲o̲f̲ ̲s̲t̲a̲r̲s̲. For the f̲i̲r̲s̲t̲ ̲t̲i̲m̲e̲, astronomers can view "w̲h̲i̲t̲e̲ ̲d̲w̲a̲r̲f̲s̲" by looking at a picture of a s̲t̲a̲r̲ ̲c̲l̲u̲s̲t̲e̲r̲. White dwarfs are stars that are n̲e̲a̲r̲ ̲t̲h̲e̲ ̲e̲n̲d̲ ̲o̲f̲ ̲t̲h̲e̲i̲r̲ ̲l̲i̲v̲e̲s̲. In addition to dying stars, astronomers are also seeing v̲e̲r̲y̲ ̲y̲o̲u̲n̲g̲ ̲s̲t̲a̲r̲s̲. We will also learn many new things about c̲o̲m̲e̲t̲s̲, p̲l̲a̲n̲e̲t̲s̲, g̲a̲l̲a̲x̲i̲e̲s̲, and even t̲h̲e̲ ̲a̲g̲e̲ ̲o̲f̲ t̲h̲e̲ ̲u̲n̲i̲v̲e̲r̲s̲e̲.

Suggestions for Generalization

Pretend you are listening to a salesperson describe the features and benefits of six different videotape playback systems. How will you organize the facts as you listen? How could a key word strategy help you recall information? How will you remember the features and decide what to buy?

Pretend you are in a phone booth calling directory assistance information. You don't have a pen to write down the number you are requesting. Describe a memory strategy to recall the number long enough to dial it correctly at least two or three times. After all, it may be busy the first time you dial.

Creation of the World According to Norse Mythology

Reference: Mythology. (1962). In *The World Book encyclopedia* (Vol. 12, p. 815). Chicago: Field Enterprises.

Orienting the Listener

Very, very early in history, people were curious about how we got here. We have answers now that are different from the answers that others have had. Here is an ancient story of the creation of the world. The story is from Norway. We call it a myth.

Additional Memory Strategies: Organization; Knowledge Base

There is a sequence in this article. It moves from the formation of the steam, to the ice, to the giant and the cow, to the first god, and finally to the creation of the world. The story may be difficult because it is so unfamiliar; many people have little knowledge base for this story. It is easier to remember information about which we already have knowledge.

(A good strategy for improving listening for lectures is to have the listeners read the information before the instructor presents it. In this way, they have some knowledge base to which to relate the material. In addition, any misconceptions can be clarified during the lecture. This can be discussed with the listener and can be practiced.)

The Information (45 Facts)

In the beginning, there was n<u>o world</u>. There was a <u>dark</u> and <u>misty</u> area to the <u>north</u> and a <u>bright</u> and <u>fiery</u> place to the <u>south</u>. <u>Between</u> these two areas was a huge, huge <u>hole</u>. <u>Twelve</u> <u>rivers</u> flowed <u>from the cool</u>, misty north. The rivers f<u>ell into</u> the hole. They <u>froze</u> in the hole. The <u>fire</u> from the south turned the ice into <u>steam</u>. The steam r<u>ose up</u> and formed an e<u>vil giant</u> named <u>Ymir</u>. He was the first giant and was the <u>father of all</u> other giants.

The <u>steam</u> also formed a <u>cow</u>. The cow <u>gave milk</u> to the giant so that he had food. The c<u>ow licked salt</u> off the ice in the hole. That was her food.

As she licked the ice, she <u>uncovered</u> the <u>first god</u>. His name was <u>Bori</u>. As time passed, Bori had children and then grandchildren. B<u>ori's three</u> <u>grandsons</u> <u>killed</u> the wicked giant Ymir.

The grandsons then <u>formed the world</u> out of the dead giant. His <u>muscles and sk</u>in became the <u>land</u>. His <u>blood</u> became the <u>waters</u>. His <u>bones</u> became the <u>rocks</u>. His <u>skull</u> formed the <u>skies</u>, and they scattered his <u>brain</u> to make the <u>clouds</u>. Then the grandsons took pieces of the <u>fire</u> of the south to make the <u>stars</u>, the <u>moon</u>, and the <u>sun</u>.

Suggestions for Generalization

Let's imagine you are in a city that you do not know well (in this example Boston, but feel free to choose another to fit the interest of the participant). You are riding public transportation. You ask the driver how to get to Fenway Park where the Red Sox play. The driver says to ride the green line to Kenmore stop. (In Boston, different routes are identified by colors.) The map shows that you will have to go to five stops. They are Boylston, Arlington, Copley, Auditorium, and Kenmore. What will you memorize and how will you do it?

Tropical Treetops

Reference: Perry, D. (1980, June). An arboreal naturalist explores the rain forest's mysterious canopy. *Smithsonian, 11*(3), 43–53.

Orienting the Listener

To understand this article, you need to know about tropical weather, rain forests, and Costa Rica. (Discuss the tropics and rain forests. Look up Costa Rica on a map. Use the map in Appendix G, if desired.) In Costa Rica, the temperature is 80° Fahrenheit and the humidity is 80 percent. Costa Rica has a large rain forest.

Additional Memory Strategies: Key Words; Organization

For this article, you may want to write down one key word for each paragraph. The choice of key words could be made by you or with help. The key words can then be used in retelling the information.

To recall information in *Tropical Treetops,* an organizational strategy can be useful. I will point out the organization as I read the article.

The Information (41 Facts)

In a tropical rain forest, the trees and vines grow very close together. (Point out that this first paragraph is a description of the setting.) The limbs of the trees often connect with one another. The vines also weave together and form a <u>connection</u>. It is so <u>thick and green</u> all year round that very little sunlight reaches the forest floor. This leafy part of the rain forest is called the <u>canopy</u>.

Until a few years ago, <u>people did not know</u> what was happening up in the canopy. They couldn't see up that high, and no one had been up there. (Tell listeners this second paragraph is a description of the problem.)

(Point out that this next paragraph is an introduction to the solution.) An inventive scientist found a way to explore the canopy in C<u>osta Rica</u>. His name is <u>Donald Perry</u>. The canopy started <u>30 feet</u> above the ground and went up to <u>150 feet</u>. Mr. Perry decided to live up in the canopy. He lived on a <u>platform</u> in the tree branches. The platform was <u>8 feet long</u> and <u>4 feet wide</u>. He was more than <u>100 feet above</u> the ground.

(Tell the listeners this fourth paragraph provides details of carrying out the solution.) Getting up into the canopy was tricky. He used a <u>crossbow</u> to shoot a <u>fishing line</u> over a tree. Then he used the fishing line to pull up a <u>sturdy rope</u>. He climbed the rope and built his platform.

(Point out that this next paragraph describes two other problems.) He had other problems to deal with. At night he wore a safety belt that was tied to a tree. That way he wouldn't "fall out of bed" and down 100 feet. Storms also were a problem. There was no way he could protect himself from the danger of tropical storms. He would listen as the trees creaked and swayed. When one tree fell, it would knock others down. Luckily, his tree never fell.

(Tell the listeners that the rest of the article discusses results.) The adventure was worthwhile. Mr. Perry was the first person to observe the life that was up in the canopy. Animals live in different places up there. For instance, he found earthworms living in dirt on the branches.

Other animals made paths along the branches. The paths went through the thick tangle of plants. There were paths for ants and ones for monkeys.

He found animals living in another place. In a hollow tree, he found cockroaches that were 3 inches long. He found crickets, scorpions, a snake, and bats in the hollow tree, too.

There were flying animals, too. He saw bees, dragonflies, butterflies, and mosquitoes that were the size of quarters.

Suggestions for Generalization

Do you ever have to write short stories in English class? Do you ever find yourself telling someone else about a movie you just saw? Memorizing the basic elements that make up a story structure will help you to organize your writing or speaking. The basic components are (1) the setting and characters; (2) the problem; (3) attempts to solve the problem; and (4) a solution to the problem. (Use whatever story structure terminology you would like.) Remember these the next time you tell, retell, or write a story to assure that you don't leave anything out.

Exploring a River

Reference: Porter, E., and Powell, J. (1969). *Down the Colorado: Diary of the first trip through the Grand Canyon* (pp. 120–121). New York: Dutton.

Orienting the Listener

I'm going to tell you about an adventure that happened in our country more than 100 years ago. To appreciate it, you will need to understand what the land was like back then. We will be talking about the west, where the canyons are so big that someone could drop the Empire State Building in one and you wouldn't know where to start looking for it. We're talking about canyons that have a river at the bottom, and in places the river becomes a waterfall. In other places, water races through rocks so fast that they churn the water making it look white and foamy. The white-water areas are called rapids because the water moves so quickly. The river races through huge rocks, tossing things around. If a boat hits a rock, it could be smashed. When boats go through the rapids, it is called "running the rapids."

The river I will talk about was unmapped. There were no cars in those days to drive explorers to the river. There were no airplanes to fly over the canyon and take pictures.

A group of men made a trip down this unmapped river. No one had ever survived this trip, although a few had tried parts of it and some had died. It is a very long trip.

We'll start with some quotes from a diary. Remember, this is a true account. Use your imagination to remember it, to picture it, to feel it. Ready? You don't have to remember this first part, but it will give you an idea of what it was like for the men. I will read quotes from the diary of John Wesley Powell.

We have had rain, from time to time, all day, and have been thoroughly drenched and chilled; but between showers the sun shines with great power, and the mercury in our thermometer stands at 115°, so that we have rapid changes from great extremes, which are very disagreeable. It is especially cold in the rain tonight. The little canvas we have is rotten and useless; the rubber ponchos, with which we started from Green River City, have all been lost; more than half the party is without hats, and not one of us has an entire suit of clothes.

After dinner, in running a rapids, the pioneer boat is upset by a wave. We are some distance in advance of the larger boats, the river is rough and swift, and we are unable to land, but cling to the boat, and are carried downstream, over another rapids. The men in the boats above see our trouble, but they are caught in whirlpools, and are spinning about in eddies, and it seems a long time before they come to our relief. At last they do come; our boat is turned right side up, bailed out...

Additional Memory Strategy: Knowledge Base

Knowing about rivers, rapids, and what it feels like to explore a river without a map will help you visualize and recall the events in this article.

The Information (60 Facts)

John Wesley Powell led a group of men down <u>600 miles</u> of river. The river starts in the <u>lower part of Wyoming</u> and goes through the whole length of <u>Utah</u> and across <u>much of Arizona</u>. The date was <u>1869</u>.

<u>Native American</u>s thought that no one could go down the river and survive. <u>Explorers</u> told stories of <u>waterfalls</u> and of powerful <u>whirlpools</u> that pulled people to their deaths. Some thought the <u>river disappeared</u> and went underground for hundreds of miles.

On <u>May 24</u>, <u>10 men</u> set out. They had <u>four wooden boats</u>. Their leader was <u>John Wesley Powell</u>. He had only a <u>single arm</u>. He had lost his other arm in the <u>Civil War</u>. He wanted to learn about the river and the lands around it. He wanted to make a <u>map</u> of the river.

It took the men <u>13 weeks</u> to go down the river. Almost every day was a battle with the river. They never knew what was around the bend because there were no maps.

When they came to rapids or waterfalls, the men had <u>three</u> ways to get past. One way was to <u>carry</u> their boats around the difficult section of the river. Sometimes they couldn't do that because the canyon walls were so steep that they couldn't climb them. When they couldn't go around the dangerous places, they had to go through them. They had two ways they could do that. The safest way was to <u>tie a boat</u> on a long rope and let it slowly travel through the difficult part of the river. Then another boat would travel down along the rope to the first one. The boats took turns traveling through the rapids or waterfall in this way until all were through. The last way to get past a difficult section of the river was for the men to "run the rapids" in their boats. They had to get in the boats and do their best to steer around rocks and waves. The boats often capsized and their equipment and food were soaked. Some things were lost. They lost some clothes and blankets and dishes.

After only a couple of weeks, one of the boats was smashed on the rocks. Many times they lost oars. They had to chop new oars out of trees along the river. During the sixth week, one man decided to leave the trip. He had had enough adventure. They came to a valley where he could walk out.

The toughest day was probably July 24. They spent all day going over three-quarters of a mile of river. There were waterfalls, rapids, whirlpools, and great waves.

In August, they experienced the deepest and darkest part of the trip. They were in the Grand Canyon. One part of the canyon is a mile deep, and the steep canyon walls blocked much of the sunlight. Their supplies were getting low. For food they had only flour, apples, and coffee left. No one had a full suit of clothes, and there were not enough blankets to go around. They were getting discouraged. They weren't certain if they would make it out of the canyon. On August 28, three men decided to leave the river. They hiked out of the canyon. That left six men to finish the trip.

They finally came out of the canyon on August 30. They saw three white men and one Native American searching for their bodies. People thought they had died on the river.

The notes that the men made about the river were valuable. They were important notes about the formation of the land and the path of the river. All the men survived except the three men who had hiked out on August 28.

Suggestions for Generalization

Pretend you are shopping at a large mall with your uncle and decide to split up. You're in a hurry and still have five things to buy: a new CD, a birthday gift for your friend, some toothpaste, a pair of socks, and a battery for your watch. How will you remember these items? You are supposed to meet your uncle again at 3:00 at the car in the parking lot. You need to remember the parking level and name. It is 6F. How will you remember it?

Pretend you went on a long car trip with your family. How could you recall your trip, day by day, for a good friend?

Dinosaurs

Reference: Battaglia, C. (1979, April). Dinosaurs are.... *Johns Hopkins Magazine*, 20–27.

Orienting the Listener

This information is a challenge to the usual theory about dinosaurs. Since dinosaurs are extinct, no one really knows what they were like. We have theories. People have found dinosaur eggs, bones, and footprints. One theory or guess that scientists have made is that dinosaurs were cold-blooded. Cold-blooded animals like frogs, snakes, and lizards cannot warm themselves. They feel cold to us. Warm-blooded animals can keep themselves warm. We are warm-blooded. So are dogs, mice, rabbits, and many other animals.

Additional Memory Strategies: Counting; Key Words

I am going to tell you information about a newer dinosaur theory. You will hear descriptions of bones. Picture what I am telling you. It will help you to remember. I will tell you that there are three reasons for this theory. Whenever you hear someone say that a certain number of facts will follow, pay careful attention. Listen for the facts. Count them. That will help you remember them. You may also want to use key words to remember the three reasons.

The Information (15 Facts)

Bob Bakker is a young scientist with new ideas about dinosaurs. He believes that dinosaurs were really warm-blooded animals like us. Dr. Bakker has many reasons for believing dinosaurs were warm-blooded. We will look at only three reasons. The ones we will talk about have to do with dinosaur bones. Dr. Bakker compared dinosaur bones with the bones of warm- and cold-blooded animals.

Do you remember ever looking at a tree that has been cut down? Remember the rings that show each year a tree has grown? Bones of warm-blooded animals have growth rings like a tree. Cold-blooded animals usually don't have growth rings. Dinosaur bones have these rings.

A second reason to believe in this new theory is that warm-blooded animals have many blood vessels in their bones. When the animals die, these blood vessels leave holes in the bone. We can see these holes where blood vessels have been. Dinosaur bones have many holes, like those of warm-blooded animals.

The third reason will take some concentration for you to understand. Ready? We know that calcium is important in bones. That's why we drink milk as children, while our bones are growing. In the bones of warm-blooded animals, calcium phosphate is deposited. It then dissolves and is redeposited over and over. These deposits leave "haversian canals" in the bones. Haversian canals are rare in cold-blooded animals but are common in warm-blooded animals. As you can guess, haversian canals are common in the bones of dinosaurs.

There's much more to Dr. Bakker's theory than I have told you, but you have much to remember already. Tell me (or write down) what you remember. I will ask questions to help jog your memory if you need it.

Suggestions for Generalization

Pretend you are a student in a social studies class. You have to remember that Belfast is the capital of Northern Ireland, where Protestants live, and Dublin is the capital of Ireland, where Catholics live. You keep getting them mixed up when you study. How can you connect Belfast, Northern Ireland, and Protestants using visualization and association? Remember to add action and absurdity to your association to help you remember.

Pretend that your supervisor just told you about a change in the computer system at work. You must now log on to your computer differently and use two new passwords. How will you remember?

Iceman

Reference: Roberts, D. (1993, June). The iceman, lone voyager from the copper age. *National Geographic*, 183(6), 36–65.

Orienting the Listener

What do you think it was like to live thousands of years ago? An amazing discovery gave us some new answers to that question. This discovery happened in the Alps. Do you know what the Alps are and where they are? This is about a man who died in the Alps.

Additional Memory Strategies: Key Words

Listening for key words is a very good way to help you recall information. As you listen to this information, find key words to help you remember.

The Information (37 facts)

The man was walking through the <u>Alps</u>, a mountain range in <u>Europe</u>. He carried a few pieces of <u>charcoal</u> to build a <u>fire</u>. Making a fire would have been difficult that night, because he was <u>too high in the mountains to gather</u> any sticks. He was at an elevation of <u>10,530</u> <u>feet</u>.

He had a long <u>bow</u>. Only two of his <u>14</u> <u>arrows</u> were <u>ready to be used</u>. He had a <u>dagger</u>. He had o<u>ther tool</u>s as well.

His food was <u>meat</u> from an <u>animal he had hunted</u>. He also had a few <u>berries</u>. He wore simple <u>leather shoe</u>s with <u>grass inside</u> to keep his feet <u>warm</u>. He had clothes made of <u>animal skin</u>s and a <u>cape</u> made of <u>grass</u>. He had w<u>avy dark hair</u> and a <u>beard</u>. He lay down to <u>sleep but died</u>. S<u>now covered</u> him.

A <u>German</u> man and woman named <u>Helmut</u> and <u>Erika</u> <u>Simon</u> found the man about <u>5,000</u> <u>years</u> later. They were hiking in the Alps on <u>September 19, 1991</u>. Erika saw his h<u>ead sticking out of the snow</u> and thought it was a <u>doll</u>. He had been frozen under the snow all that time.

Suggestions for Generalization

Pretend you are taking care of your neighbor's children. The parents have written down the emergency phone numbers and left them by the phone because emergency numbers are too important to leave to memory. They tell you that the children have to be in pajamas by 8:00. They say you can read the children Chapter 5 in *The Velveteen Rabbit*. Lights are to be out at 8:30. If Uncle Charlie calls, you are to tell him they'll be home by 11:00. How can you remember all of that?

Pretend that, a year ago, you witnessed a car accident. Now you have been subpoenaed to appear in court to testify about what you saw. Use key words to organize your account of the accident.

California

Reference: California. (1980). In *Colliers encyclopedia* (Vol. 5, pp. 152–173). New York: Macmillan.

Orienting the Listener

When you think of California, what do you think of? (Pursue the discussion for a short time.) There is so much variety in California that it is hard to imagine. I'm going to describe some of the variety so that you will understand it better. Then when you hear things about it, you can fit that information in with what you know. It will make more sense to you.

Additional Memory Strategy: Knowledge Base

Information I read to you about California will be better retained if you have some knowledge about this state. The knowledge you already have about California will help you remember new information about it.

The Information (53 Facts)

(For this article, duplicate the *Master Map of California* on page 100, and display it as you read about California. Also duplicate the *Map of California* on page 101 for each listener and distribute the maps to them after reading the article.) First, let me show you San Francisco and Los Angeles on the map, because you hear much about these cities. Here is San Francisco, and here is Los Angeles (using the map on page 100, point to these places). They are about 400 miles apart. It would take a day to drive from one to the other. They are very different. Los Angeles is a huge city that is spread out. The land is quite flat. Hollywood and Disneyland are in the Los Angeles area.

San Francisco is built on hills overlooking the ocean and San Francisco Bay. It covers a smaller area. Houses are close together. It is cool in the summer and mild in the winter. It doesn't snow in San Francisco or in Los Angeles. (Imagine visiting these places. Picture yourself in that weather.)

There are several mountain ranges in California, and some are along the coast. The Coastal mountains (point) are not as tall as the Sierra mountains. They get up to 9,000–10,000 feet high in the north (point) and south (point) along the coast.

These two Xs in the north (point) mark mountains that are volcanic. They are in the Cascade range. Mt. Shasta (point) here in the north is a little more than 14,000 feet high. Mt. Lassen (point) is about 10,500 feet high. Mt. Lassen had minor eruptions from 1914 to 1917.

Now we move on to the Sierra Nevada mountains. They stretch from here to here (point). They are not volcanic. They are made of granite. Yosemite National Park is about here (point). It is known for its beautiful, tall waterfalls. The Sierras are the tallest California mountains. Mt. Whitney (point) is about 14,500 feet tall and is the tallest mountain in the continental United States.

We have the highest point in the U.S. here (point), and the lowest is not far away. The lowest is in Death Valley. It is 282 feet below sea level (point). All of this area is desert (point). This is Death Valley (point), and this is the Mojave Desert (point). Sometimes it doesn't rain for years here.

Going down the middle of California is a valley called the Central Valley (point). I'm sure you've heard about the redwood trees in California. There are two kinds there. The coastal kind goes from here to here (point). The coastal kind is the tallest redwood. It needs the ocean fog to survive.

The redwoods that are the widest are the ones in the Sierra Mountains. "Big Tree," the largest known redwood, is about here (point). It is 36 and one-half feet in diameter.

Now, using your map of California, write down the names of cities, mountains, valleys, and so forth. Write down the numbers that you can remember. Also, remember to describe the cities and trees. Organize your information however you want, but make it clear so I can tell that you know the information.

Suggestions for Generalization

Estimate the size of "Big Tree." For instance, how many rooms would the tree fill? How many people would be able to line up around it if they were to lie head to toe in a circle? This type of thinking is helpful in giving meaning to numbers, which in turn makes other numbers you hear more meaningful. Think of other situations when giving meaning to numbers helps you to remember them better.

Master Map of California

Mt. Shasta 14,000'+ (14,162')

Mt. Lassen about 10,500' (10,466')

Yosemite National Park

Cascade Sierra Nevada

Central Valley

San Francisco

Big Tree

Mt. Whitney 14,495'

Death Valley

Coastal Redwoods
from here north

-282'

Mojave Desert

Los Angeles

 © 1997 Thinking Publications. Duplication permitted for educational use only.

Map of California

_____

_____

_____

_____

_____

_____

_____

_____

_____

© 1997 Thinking Publications. Duplication permitted for educational use only.

Section IV

Retention and Recall of Oral Directions

Goal: The listener will recall oral directions.

Rationale

In this section, listeners learn to apply their memory strategies to remembering and following oral directions. The procedures for presentation are similar to those for the articles in Section III; therefore, most participants will find the transition to these exercises easy.

The goal of this section is to generalize strategy use to various relevant life situations. As mentioned earlier, the lessons in Section IV can be presented in tandem with Section III lessons. The order of presentation is unimportant. Pick and choose the materials and their order of presentation. These materials may stimulate ideas for additional oral directions that may be of interest to specific participants. For example, the adult providing intervention can develop directions for getting to a concert in the area, for buying tickets to a special event, for trying out for a play, or for learning a new game.

Materials

This section contains a great variety of materials. The oral directions relate to school situations, job situations, leisure activities, and projects. This variety is intended to promote generalization to listening experiences in every part of the participants' lives. Directions in the lessons are presented orally. The listener responds on paper or orally, depending on the number of participants in the group. Other directions incorporate visual materials that the listener uses before, during, and/or after the directions are presented.

Presentation

Present the lessons by orienting the listeners, discussing possible memory strategies, presenting the direction information, and then asking the listeners to recall by demonstrating the directions, by retelling them, or by writing them.

The lessons begin on page 106. Each lesson contains components similar to those in Section III, including suggestions for orienting the listeners, additional memory strategies, the direction information, and suggestions for generalization. In addition, each lesson includes a materials list that describes materials needed for the lesson. As with the other sections, the materials should be adapted to the needs and interest levels of the participants.

The additional memory strategies suggested in this section have been defined on pages 54–55. This section also includes the following memory strategies:

1. wh-questions—using wh-questions (e.g., who, what, did what, where, when, why, and how) to prompt recall of information.

2. eliminating distractions—avoiding distracting stimuli (e.g., other people, noise, internal distractors) that inhibit concentration.

The list on page 105 provides an overview of the lessons in this section. It indicates each lesson title, the number of facts to be recalled, and the additional memory strategy or strategies emphasized.

As with Section III, important facts are underlined to provide a built-in standard to measure recall. The facts primarily consist of objects, locations, people, numerical facts, and important concepts.

Monitoring Progress

In Section IV, as in Sections II and III, counting facts recalled is a way of monitoring progress. (See Section II, pages 47–49, for a description of how facts are counted.) However, in some lessons, progress can be monitored by observing whether the listener completes the directions as given. Data can be gathered during each lesson and recorded on the *Progress Sheet* provided.

Section IV Lessons

Page #	Title	No. of Facts	Additional Memory Strategies
106	*Throwing a Boomerang*	9	kinesthetic imagery
107	*Aerodynamics*	9	counting; asking for repetition
109	*Juggling*	16	kinesthetic imagery
110	*Tepee*	30	organization; key words
113	*Leaving for a Trip*	14–16	kinesthetic imagery
116	*A Play*	15	key words
119	*Burros*	13	counting
120	*Hidden Waterfall*	13	kinesthetic imagery
123	*Going to a Flea Market*	12	asking for repetition
124	*Registering a Car*	16	key words; counting
126	*Pyramid*	25	counting; organization
129	*Photo Contest*	19+	wh-questions
131	*How to Dive for Treasures*	23	organization; counting
133	*Making a Movie*	30	counting
135	*Microscope*	15	knowledge base; key words
138	*School Announcement*	7	eliminating distractions; key words
139	*Homework Assignments*	8–13	asking for repetition; key words
141	*Job Directions*	10–14	kinesthetic imagery

Throwing a Boomerang

Reference: Boomerang. (1962). In *The World Book encyclopedia* (Vol. 2, p. 393). Chicago: Field Enterprises.

Materials

None

Orienting the Listener

Have you ever tried to throw a boomerang? (Pause for responses.) I'm going to tell you how to throw a boomerang. Listen very carefully. Picture yourself doing what I say. If you picture yourself using your body, your body will help you remember what to do.

Additional Memory Strategy: Kinesthetic Imagery

While you are listening, you can imagine yourself doing these things. This is called kinesthetic imagery. You actually can touch your fingers if that helps you remember the part about holding the boomerang. You may imagine the feeling of your arm moving and the weight of the boomerang as it moves.

The Information (9 Facts)

Hold <u>either end</u> of the boomerang with <u>three</u> <u>fingers</u>. (Show listeners how you can actually touch your three fingers to help you remember.) Put it over your shoulder with the o<u>ther end</u> <u>pointing down</u>. Throw the boomerang <u>overhand</u> with your a<u>rm straight</u>. (Make a slight gesture with your hand to help listeners imagine their arms going up.) Just as you are letting it go, give it a <u>flick of your wrist</u>. That will make it <u>spin</u>. Good luck. I hope it returns.

Suggestions for Generalization

Describe four important steps to installing a computer game on your computer. Organize your thinking before presenting the information. Ask someone in the group to recall the steps. What strategy was used to remember?

Aerodynamics

Reference: Aerodynamics. (1962). In *The World Book encyclopedia* (Vol. 1, pp. 74, 77). Chicago: Field Enterprises.

Materials

1. One 3" x 5" card per participant
2. One stickpin per participant
3. One spool of thread
4. One drinking straw per participant

Orienting the Listener

Aerodynamics is the study of air as it moves around things. Movement of air around an airplane keeps the airplane in the air when it flies. You are going to do an experiment to test what happens to a card when air goes over its flat surface.

(In this lesson, a drinking straw is used to provide a sanitary yet easy way to perform this experiment with many participants. Using the same spool, each participant uses a straw and then discards it. For the experiment to work, the straw must fit snugly through the hole in the spool so that the air is directed powerfully through the opposite end. Choose a spool and straw that fit snugly, or apply masking tape to the end of the spool where the straw is inserted [opposite the pin/card end]. Then, with a pencil tip, make a hole in the tape just large enough to fit the straw snugly. After this lesson is presented, the listener demonstrates physical recall of the directions, rather than retelling or writing the directions.)

Additional Memory Strategies: Counting; Asking for Repetition

Whenever you hear someone say he or she is going to tell you three things or five things or any number of things, you know that you will hear that number of things. You can then count the things as they are presented to make sure you understand what they are and that you have not missed any. If you don't hear all of them, you can ask the speaker to repeat them or to clear up your confusion. Then, when you need to recall them, you can use counting as a strategy for remembering them.

The Information (9 Facts)

You will need three things: (1) a small <u>index card</u>; (2) a <u>stickpin</u>; and (3) a <u>spool of thread</u> with a straw in one end. (Provide the supplies to the listeners after the directions are read. The listeners can then do the experiment.)

Push the pin through the middle of the card. Leave the pin in the card. Next, pick up the spool and hold it with the straw pointing down. Put the pin into the hole in the other end of the spool. The card will be sitting on the top of the spool. The pin will go through the card and sit in the hole of the spool. Tip your head back so you can blow into the straw on the bottom of the spool. Blow hard. You can tip the spool over while you are blowing hard. What does the card do? Can you blow the card off?

The aerodynamic rule you have experimented with is that fast-moving air going over a surface makes the surface move toward the air.

Suggestions for Generalization

Describe a situation in which you have to follow directions involving manipulatives (e.g., a science experiment, assembling something purchased for your home, assembling a model car). In some cases, the memory task is not auditory but is instead from reading directions or looking at diagrams. Then, memory strategies such as the use of counting can still be useful.

Juggling

Reference: Cassidy, J., and Rembeaux, B.C. (1980). *Juggling for the complete klutz*. Stanford, CA: Klutz Press.

Materials

None

Orienting the Listener

Have you ever had the desire to juggle? Or, have you ever wondered how other people do it? Listen carefully. I will tell you the beginning steps in juggling.

Additional Memory Strategy: Kinesthetic Imagery

Because juggling is an activity that uses the body, some people could imagine their bodies moving as they listen to the directions. Later, those images help them remember what their bodies should do. This memory strategy is called kinesthetic imagery. Visualize what I say to you so that you can remember the steps. The images can take the place of remembering words. Listen carefully. Then I will ask you to tell (or write) the directions.

The Information (16 Facts)

You must start with a tennis ball to learn the technique. Stand up. Relax. Hold the ball in one hand. Hold the ball on the palm of your hand, not on your fingers. Toss the ball from one hand to the other. The ball should go as high as your eyes. It should go from one side of your body to the other side, in an arch as wide as your body. Catch the ball in the palm of your hand. Practice for a few minutes.

After tossing one ball is easy, take two balls. Hold one ball in each hand. Remember to hold them in your palms. Toss one ball as you have just learned to do. Just before you catch it in your other hand, toss the second ball up out of that hand. You will need to practice this for at least 10 minutes.

Suggestions for Generalization

Pretend you are going grocery shopping. A friend asks you get three items for her: a can of stewed tomatoes, toothpaste, and a can of green olives. You can't find a pen to write these items down. How could you remember the three items? What other situations have you been in when you had a few items to remember and couldn't write them down? What strategies could you have used to remember the items?

Tepee

Reference: Hunt, B.W. (1954). *Indian crafts and lore.* New York: Golden Press.

Materials

Tepee Diagram (See page 112; duplicate one per participant.)

Orienting the Listener

We have been practicing following directions and visualizing the steps without writing them down. This time you will look at a diagram while you imagine yourself doing this job. Some of what I say will be presented in the diagram and some will not. Remember to pay attention to all of the information. Make associations in your mind to remember the numbers. (Distribute the *Tepee Diagram* showing the steps for making a tepee.) I will describe the way to make a tepee while you look at the diagram. After I'm done, I'll take the diagram back. Remember the diagram and then tell me (or write down) how to put up a tepee.

Additional Memory Strategies: Organization; Key Words

I will present many directions in a certain order. You have to do one thing before you do another. Here are the general ideas in this presentation: You find the poles, tie them together, make a circle of them, lift the cover, fasten the cover to the poles, and then fix the smoke flaps. Remembering the order can help you recall the steps. The diagram also can help.

(For more advanced participants, ask them to identify the steps as they listen or present the article a second time and ask them to identify the steps. In addition, listeners could choose key words to represent the ideas in each step.)

The Information (30 Facts)

(Point to the diagram as you describe the steps to help clarify the directions. Stress that listeners must understand each step to remember it [i.e., we remember information best if we understand it].)

(Tell listeners that this first set of directions provides a description of the poles.) Gather <u>15</u> poles. They should be about <u>17</u> <u>feet long</u>. They should be <u>wider at the bottom</u> end and narrower at the top. They <u>should be stiff</u> so they don't bend easily. If they bend, the tepee won't stay straight.

(Tell listeners that this second set of directions describes the assembling of the first three poles.) To begin assembling the tepee, take <u>3 poles</u>. T<u>ie them</u> together n<u>ear the top</u>. Tie them very, v<u>ery firmly</u> because the poles and the rope will be holding up the whole tepee. You don't want them to slip.

(Tell listeners that the third set of directions describes the circle of poles.) <u>Stand the 3</u> poles up in a tripod formation. <u>Lean 8 more</u> poles on these 3 so that the 11 poles <u>make a circle</u>. Leave a <u>space for one</u> more pole.

(Tell listeners that the fourth set of directions describes lifting the cover.) The next job is to get the cover on. The tepee is too tall for you to reach the top so you must use another way. Tie the <u>cover onto a pole</u>. Lift the pole with the cover. A<u>dd that pole</u> to the circle of poles. P<u>ull the cover</u> around the poles. Do you see this step in the diagram?

(Tell listeners that this set of directions describes fastening the cover.) The cover is on the tepee, but it isn't fastened in front. On the two front edges there are p<u>airs of hole</u>s. The pairs of holes on the <u>right side go over</u> the pairs on the left side. Do you see this in the diagram? (Point to the close-up on the diagram.) It shows the holes going over one another. Now you can put a small <u>stick through each pa</u>ir of holes. The sticks will hold the edges of the tepee together. See the last step on the diagram? It shows all of the sticks in place. Now you have only two more things to do. You need to <u>fasten the botto</u>m of the tepee with stakes. Do you see that? You also need to fasten the smoke flaps at the top.

(Tell listeners that this set of directions describes the smoke flaps.) The s<u>moke flap</u>s are held open by <u>2 long pole</u>s. The poles go <u>through the top hole</u>s in the flaps. Then the poles c<u>ross behind the</u> tepee. <u>Ropes</u> are fastened to the two b<u>ottom hole</u>s and are <u>tied to tent stakes</u>. This holds the flap firmly. (Now remove the diagram from the view of listeners.)

Suggestions for Generalization

Pretend you are a student and you missed English class today because of a dentist appointment. You meant to get the assignment earlier but didn't. Now you are hurrying to catch your bus after school. You pass your English teacher and ask her what to do for homework. She tells you the assignment as you are running to catch the bus. What memory strategy could you use so you won't forget what to do?

Pretend you arrived late at a meeting at work. Someone stops to brief you on five decisions already made. How will you remember them?

Tepee Diagram

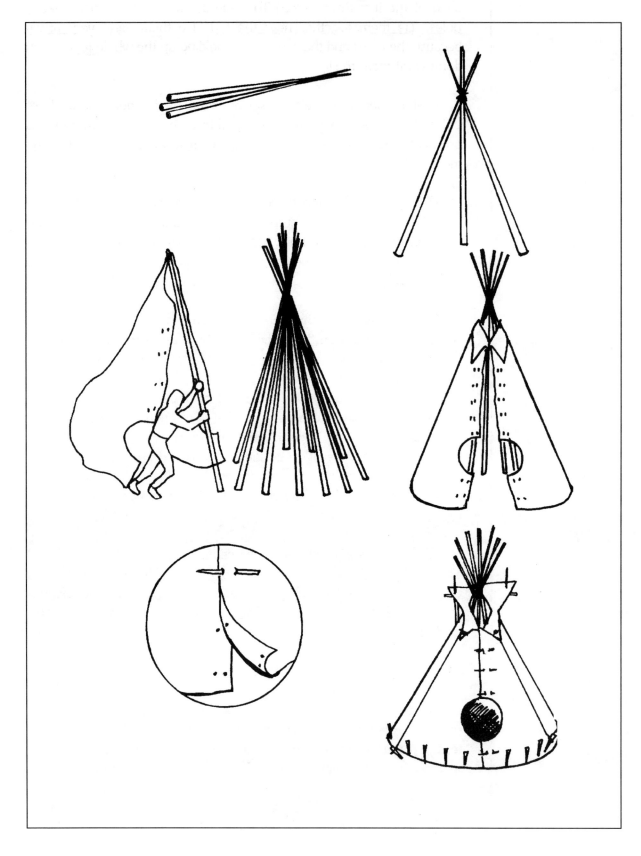

© 1997 Thinking Publications. Duplication permitted for educational use only.

Leaving for a Trip

Materials

House Diagram (See page 115; duplicate one per participant.)

Orienting the Listener

We will be pretending that you're going on a trip and your family has to work together to get ready.

Additional Memory Strategy: Kinesthetic Imagery

When you need to remember to do chores at your own home, visualizing the actions in your mind can help you remember them. Later, when you actually need to do them, your mental images of those actions help you.

Let's try visualizing being at your house. Imagine that you are in your house, standing in your kitchen. I am going to take you silently on a trip through your house. When I am done, tell me as much of the trip as you can remember.

You open the refrigerator and get something to eat from the bottom shelf. You close the refrigerator and put the item on the table. You just remembered that you left the TV on. You leave the kitchen and go to the TV. You turn it off. Someone is knocking at the door, so you go to the door and see who it is. It is your friend, whom you invite into the kitchen to share the food you put on the table. Next you walk into the basement, turn, and bend over to see what is under the stairs. You then walk up to the attic and open the door.

That is the end of your journey. Recall for me what you did. (The listeners might choose either visualization or kinesthetic images to imagine this trip through the house. It is not necessary to know which they choose, but you can discuss with listeners that imagining is a very useful way to remember an oral direction that involves action.)

The Information (14–16 Facts)

(Distribute the diagram of the house. Have participants look over the diagram so they are familiar with it. Answer any questions they might have about the diagram so they recognize the items in the drawing. Have the listeners put away the diagram before you present the information so they can concentrate on visualizing their own images.)

You're going on a family trip, and everyone needs to help get ready. You have a list of things to do to help. Visualize yourself doing them. Picture yourself in these rooms, seeing these things, and doing these jobs. (Assign each participant one of the following lists of jobs.)

Person 1:

<u>Sh</u>ut the <u>window</u> a<u>bove the dryer</u> <u>in the basement</u>.	(3 facts)
Turn the h<u>eat down</u> to <u>50 degrees</u>.	(3 facts)
Get the <u>toothbrushes</u> <u>from the bathroom</u>. <u>Put</u> them o<u>n your dresser</u>.	(4 facts)
Bring down <u>two</u> <u>suitcases</u> <u>from the attic</u>. <u>Put</u> them i<u>n the bedroo</u>m.	(5 facts)

(15 Facts)

Person 2:

There's a <u>key hanging</u> b<u>y the kitchen door</u>. T<u>ake it</u> over t<u>o the neighbors</u>.	(4 facts)
<u>Water</u> the <u>plants</u> i<u>n the living room</u> and i<u>n the kitchen</u>.	(4 facts)
<u>Close</u> the <u>curtains</u> i<u>n the living roo</u>m.	(3 facts)
<u>Put</u> the <u>cat</u> in the basement. Give her <u>food</u> and <u>water</u>.	(5 facts)

(16 Facts)

Person 3:

Check the <u>stove</u> to make certain i<u>t is of</u>f.	(2 facts)
There is a b<u>ag of foo</u>d <u>in the refrigerator</u>. <u>Put it in the car</u>.	(4 facts)
There's a b<u>ag of tras</u>h <u>in the kitchen</u>. Take it out and <u>put it into the garbage can</u>.	(4 facts)
There are <u>three</u> <u>letters</u> b<u>y the TV</u>. <u>Mail</u> them.	(4 facts)

(14 Facts)

Person 4:

There's a stack of <u>clothes</u> o<u>n the bed</u> in the <u>children's room</u>. P<u>ack it</u>.	(4 facts)
There's <u>rope</u> <u>in the box</u> u<u>nder the basement stair</u>s. <u>Put</u> the rope <u>in the car</u>.	(5 facts)
Get the <u>clothes</u> o<u>ut of the dryer</u>. <u>Put</u> them in <u>your bedroo</u>m.	(4 facts)
<u>Unplug</u> the <u>TV</u>.	(2 facts)

(15 Facts)

Suggestions for Generalization

What jobs does your family need you to help with? Are they the same every week? What strategies could you use to remember what to do? Share an experience from your life that demonstrates use of a memory strategy.

House Diagram

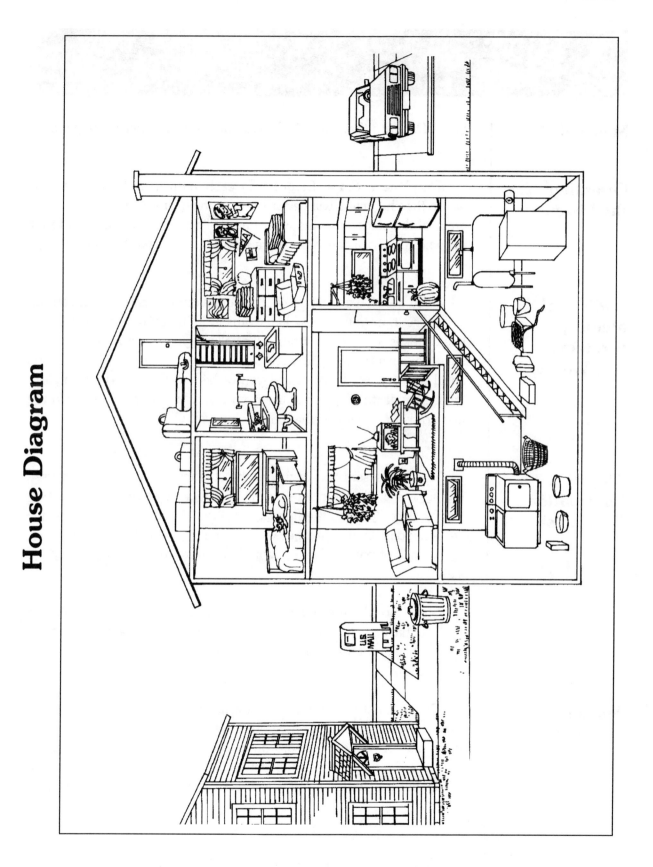

© 1997 Thinking Publications. Duplication permitted for educational use only.

A Play

Materials

Stage Diagram (See page 118; duplicate one copy per participant.)

Orienting the Listener

(Distribute a *Stage Diagram* to each participant.) I will describe where the characters will be for the beginning of a play. Here is a diagram of the stage. Imagine what I am telling you. I will ask you to tell me who the characters are, where they are, and what they are doing.

Additional Memory Strategy: Key Words

If you ever have to do an oral presentation, you can read it, you can memorize it, or you can use key words to help you remember it. Using key words is a powerful strategy that allows you to remember a whole idea. For example, if you were talking about Thomas Jefferson, you could use key words to remind you of his childhood, his accomplishments, his death. If you had to give a talk at a meeting, you could use key words to remember the main points you want to say.

The Information (15 Facts)

This is a description of where the characters are on the stage set. Mother is seated on the sofa staring at a book of photos. Father is pacing the floor between the fireplace and the telephone. The police officer is standing by the fireplace with one hand on the mantle. He is holding a piece of paper. The 15-year-old daughter enters from behind the sofa.

Show me where everyone is and what they are doing. (An alternative is to have the listeners write on the diagram who the characters are, where they are, and what they are doing.)

Suggestions for Generalization

Pretend that you are in a performance. One part of your performance is difficult to get in the right order. The rest of it is easy and you don't need to work extra hard on it. But this one part makes you nervous, because you are afraid you will do it wrong. How could you remember it? The following is the scenario you will need to remember (choose one):

Situation 1: You are a detective solving a crime. At the end of the first act, you turn to the photographer and ask, "Why did you change your clothes before you came back downstairs after dinner?" Then the curtain falls.

At the end of the first scene of Act II, you turn to the cook and say, "Why did you change the menu for the dinner tonight?"

Situation 2: In a concert, you are singing in a group. There are four verses. Each time you get to the chorus, one word is changed. The first time you are supposed to sing, "And gave it to the handyman." Next you are supposed to sing, "And gave it to the dairyman." The third time you need to sing, "And gave it to the bogeyman." For the last verse, you are supposed to sing, "And gave it to us, every man."

Stage Diagram

 © 1997 Thinking Publications. Duplication permitted for educational use only.

Burros

Reference: Garrett, W.E. (1978). Grand canyon: Are we loving it to death? *National Geographic, 154*(1), pp. 16–31.

Materials

None

Orienting the Listener

The first burros were brought to the Grand Canyon by prospectors looking for gold. The prospectors left, but many burros stayed. The burros kept multiplying. They caused problems in the canyon. There aren't many plants in the canyon. The burros ate many of the plants. That made it harder for the native bighorn sheep and mule deer to find food. The burros also caused erosion with their trails, and they wrecked old archeological sites where the Native Americans had lived. Your job is to help take the burros out of the canyon. Here is how you do it.

Additional Memory Strategy: Counting

When you hear a speaker use the word *first*, you know there is usually a list coming. In this case, I won't use *second* or *third*, but there are three things to which you should pay attention. Do you want me to tell you the three things, or do you want to listen for them?

The Information (13 Facts)

First, you must capture the burro. You will shoot it with a special dart. The dart is called an immobilizing dart. It makes the burro sleep. One danger is that the burro may stop breathing, so you may have to administer artificial respiration, or "mouth-to-muzzle" resuscitation, to get the burro breathing again.

You have a special bag to put the burro in. The bag is made of net. Put the burro in the bag. Tie a long rope to the bag. Attach the other end of the rope to the bottom of a helicopter. The helicopter will fly out of the canyon with the burro hanging down under it. Your part of the job is done.

Suggestions for Generalization

Pretend you're in the mall and need to use the restroom. You ask a clerk for directions. Here is what you have to remember: Go out of the store and walk until you see the shoe store on your left. Turn right and go past two stores. Just before you get to the pizza shop, turn right. At the end of that hall are the restrooms. What memory strategy would you use to remember these directions?

Hidden Waterfall

Materials

Map to Waterfall (See page 122; duplicate one per participant.)

Orienting the Listener

(To prepare the listeners for this lesson, go over the symbols on the map. Do not show participants the map until after they have heard the directions. Make certain that participants know their right and left, or they will not be able to do this lesson. An indication of listener success is whether or not they reach the waterfall. In this lesson, counting facts may be irrelevant.)

The symbols on the map are:

trails ----------   rock

    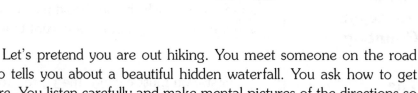

cabin   lake

Let's pretend you are out hiking. You meet someone on the road who tells you about a beautiful hidden waterfall. You ask how to get there. You listen carefully and make mental pictures of the directions so you can find your way on the trail. I will read the directions to you. Then you will look at a drawing of the area. You will figure out where the waterfall is and show that place to me.

Additional Memory Strategy: Kinesthetic Imagery

As you listen, you may find it helpful to imagine you are turning in the direction that I tell you. For instance, if you are told to turn left after the houses, imagine yourself turning left and reaching out toward the houses with your left hand.

The Information (13 Facts)

You are on a road. Keep going <u>down the road</u>. There are <u>two cabins close together</u>. When you see them, <u>look for the trail</u>. It is just <u>past the cabins</u>.

Soon after you get on the trail, the trail splits. Take the <u>left fork—</u> the trail on the left.

You will follow that trail until you come to another fork. You will see a <u>lake there</u>. Take the <u>right-hand trail</u>. Keep the lake on your left. Go <u>partway around</u> the lake.

After the trail leaves the lake, keep going. You will come to one more fork. Just after <u>you go through</u> a beautiful stand of <u>tall trees</u>, you will see a <u>huge rock</u>. Turn <u>left</u> by the rock. Follow that trail. It will end at the waterfall.

Now, here is the map. Follow the trail, and tell me where the waterfall is.

Suggestions for Generalization

Pretend you are in the center of town (choose a place). Your friend just discovered that he lost his wallet. He wants to find it quickly before anyone else finds it. You decide to split up to look for it. How can you remember the places you are supposed to look? (Note: An actual description of a store, mall, or shopping district that is familiar to everyone could be used.)

Map to Waterfall

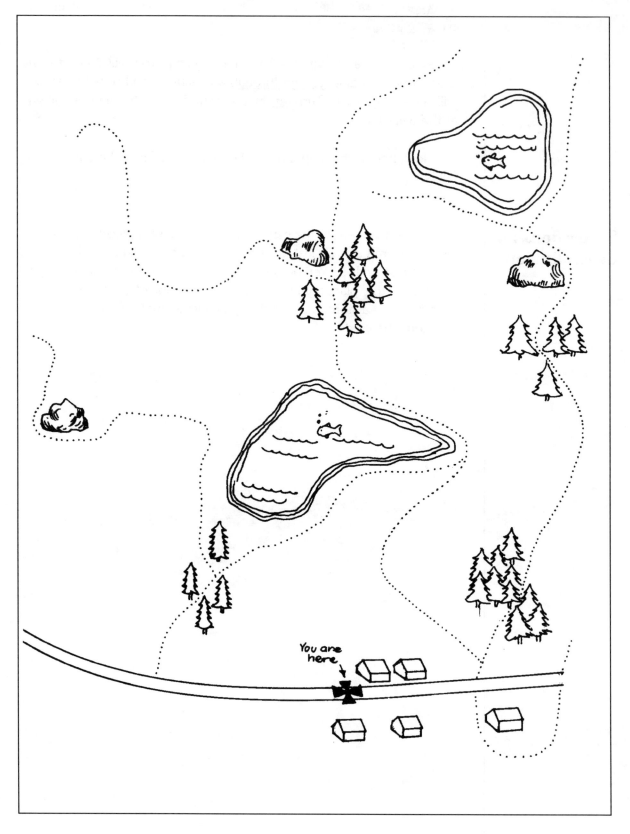

© 1997 Thinking Publications. Duplication permitted for educational use only.

Going to a Flea Market

Materials

None

Orienting the Listener

A friend tells you about a really good flea market. You want to go. The friend tells you how to get there. You'd like to write it down, but neither of you has a pencil or paper. So, you try to remember what he tells you, using as many strategies as you can.

Additional Memory Strategy: Asking for Repetition

Directions can be very important, as you know if you've ever gotten lost. Since these directions are complicated, you may need to ask for them to be repeated. That is fine. If you were trying to find a real place based on directions from a stranger or friend, you would want to ask for a repetition because you don't want to end up in the wrong place. Also, if the information is presented too quickly, it is fine to ask the person to repeat it more slowly. There are many ways to ask. Can you think of a few?

The Information (12 Facts)

Take Route 9N to 295. When you get to Springfield, take the Congress Street exit. Follow Congress Street. At the third traffic light, turn right. The first street you will come to is Virginia Street. Turn left on Virginia Street. Go a half mile. You will see the flea market on your left.

Suggestions for Generalization

People tell each other directions a lot. Many people ask for directions around this building. I am often asked, "How do you get to room 219?" At other times, people tell the way to someone's house or to a baseball or football game. Pretend you've asked me for directions. Just for fun, I'm going to keep the destination a secret. Listen and see if you can tell where it is. (Give directions to a place within the building or within the town. Have participants take turns giving directions also.)

Registering a Car

Materials

None

**Orienting
the Listener**

When you buy a car, you have to register it with the government. When you register it, you go through several steps. You would find out the steps by calling your state department of motor vehicles or your car insurance company. Remember, when you call a company or government agency, it's the job of the person on the phone to help you. Feel free to ask questions. Take notes, slow the person down if he or she talks too fast, and have information repeated if you need to. Just for practice, when I tell you about registering a car, try to get the information the first time if you can. If you feel lost, though, I'll repeat or clarify the information.

In this activity, pretend you see a used car that you want to buy. You've never owned a car before. You call for information about how to register the car. Listen carefully and write down the information I tell you (or tell me the steps) when I'm done. (Be aware that not all agencies have the same registration procedures. Tell listeners that the procedure outlined below may vary in their location, or modify the lesson to reflect local policies.)

**Additional
Memory
Strategies:
Key Words;
Counting**

You will be going to different places in the process of getting your registration. You can use key words and counting to help keep track of the places. It might help you to think "Where am I?" and "How many things do I need to do here?" First, you will be with the car owner, from whom you need to get five pieces of information. Key words could be *owner* and *five*. Second, you will be at the insurance company. Key words could be *insurance company*, *money*, and *form*. Third, you will be at the state department of motor vehicles. Key words could be *state*, *form*, *money*, and *license plate*. Fourth, you again will be with the car owner. Key words could be *money* and *title*.

**The
Information
(16 Facts)**

You have found a car that you like. You need to get information from the owner. Write down the make, model, and year of the car. The make means the company that made the car (e.g., Ford, Chrysler, etc.). The model tells you if it's a minivan, a sedan, and so forth. The year is the year the car was made. Also, get the title number and serial number. The title proves who owns the car. Each car has its own serial number printed on it.

Next, go to the insurance company. Take the information about the car to the company. People there will help you choose how much insurance you need. You shouldn't own a car without insurance. You will have to leave a down payment with the insurance company, so bring some money or a checkbook. The insurance company gives you a form to fill out.

Take the form from the insurance company to the state department of motor vehicles. Someone there will take your insurance form. You pay the department a fee for your registration and sales tax. You then will receive your license plate(s) in the mail in a few weeks and can put them on your car.

After leaving the motor vehicles department, go back to the owner. Pay the rest of the money you owe for the car. The owner will sign the title over to you, and you now own the car.

Suggestions for Generalization

In some areas, a phone number can be called for a weather prediction. If you live in such an area, call this number and practice using memory strategies to remember the report. (A tape recording of a forecast from the radio or one from the day's paper can also be used.) What strategies work best when you can't ask questions or ask for information to be repeated?

Pyramid

Reference: Pyramid. (1962). In *The World Book encyclopedia* (Vol. 14, pp. 809–811). Chicago: Field Enterprises.

Materials

Diagram of a Pyramid (See page 128; duplicate one per participant.)

Orienting the Listener

You are going to pretend to build a great pyramid like the ones in Egypt. Listen very carefully to my directions and study the *Diagram of a Pyramid* I give to you so you will know how to build it. There will be several numbers in what I read, so be certain to remember them. Recall as much information as you can when I'm done. (Distribute the pyramid diagrams.)

Additional Memory Strategies: Counting; Organization

Oral directions usually have several steps. Can one of you tell me how to fix a flat tire (make cookies, open a combination lock)? The rest of us will try to listen for the steps. Two strategies you could use to help you remember the steps are to count the steps or to organize the information. Listen to this set of directions and see which strategy works best for you.

The Information (25 Facts)

First, clear the ground for the pyramid. Clear a square piece of land the size of eight football fields.

Now, cut the stone blocks that you will use to build the pyramid. Cut two and one-half million stone blocks. Each will weigh about two and one-half tons.

Now you're ready. Fill up the square of ground that you cleared. Lay stone blocks side by side until the whole area is covered. As you can see from the diagram, you do need to leave one small hole free for the passageway that slopes down from the entrance.

On top of the first layer, put a second layer of blocks. Keep piling up layers of stone blocks. The pyramid will be almost solid stone when you're done. You will leave just a few passageways and a couple of rooms. Each new layer going up is just a little smaller than the one below it.

The <u>entrance</u> is about <u>55</u> <u>feet up</u> on the <u>north side</u> of the pyramid. You go down the passageway and then up again to get to a small room. The <u>small roo</u>m is the <u>queen's chamber</u>.

Keep piling on more stone blocks until you reach <u>150</u> <u>fee</u>t. Leave space at 150 feet for the <u>king's chamber</u>. Keep adding more and more layers until you get up to the top. It will be about <u>450</u> <u>feet hig</u>h. That's about as tall as a <u>40</u>-s<u>tory building</u>.

Suggestions for Generalization

Pretend you are a coach on a baseball team. You have just changed the batting order because one of the team members isn't playing today. How can you remember the following four names in order? (Note: Include names that are generally heard around your location.)

Diagram of a Pyramid

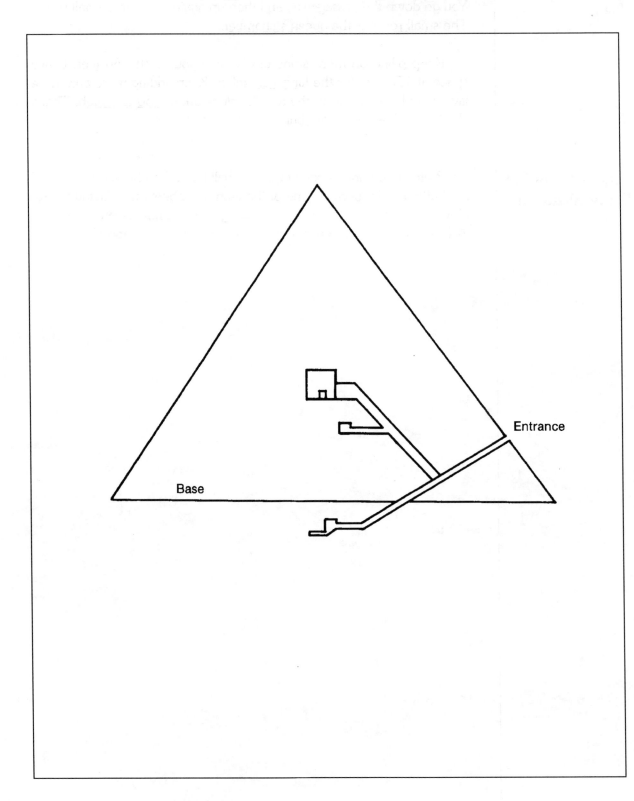

Entrance

Base

© 1997 Thinking Publications. Duplication permitted for educational use only.

Photo Contest

Materials

None

Orienting the Listener

In this lesson, you are going to pretend that you are a photographer. You want to enter a photo contest. There are many rules.

Additional Memory Strategy: Wh-Questions

Sometimes when you are stuck and can't remember something, asking yourself a list of one-word questions may help you recall those things you have forgotten. The questions you could ask yourself are: who, what, did what, where, when, why, and how.

The Information (19+ Facts)

(Feel free to simplify and to omit information at your discretion, but don't underestimate the listener's skills. Make it challenging. More than 19 facts can be counted if the list of prices is recalled.) This is a color photography contest. The prizes are:

> First Prize $1,000
> Second Prize $500
> Third Prize $250
> Fourth Prize $100
> Youth Award $50
> Honor Award $25

1. To enter, you have to be an <u>amateur photographer</u>. That means you don't earn your living by taking pictures.

2. You must <u>live in the state of New York</u>. (Substitute a listener's home location.)

3. You may send o<u>nly one photograph</u>.

4. The photograph may be a <u>print or slide</u> of <u>any size</u>. You must be able to <u>provide the negative</u> for a print.

5. The photo may be from <u>anyplace</u> in the world.

6. The photo must have been taken after <u>July 1</u>. It must not be entered in an<u>y other photo contest</u>.

7. You m<u>ay trim</u> the photo, but you <u>cannot combin</u>e photos to make one picture.

8. Print your <u>name,</u> <u>address,</u> <u>phone number</u>, and a <u>title</u> <u>on the back of the photo</u>. If you are <u>younger than 16</u>, <u>put your age</u> on the back also.

Suggestions for Generalization

(Ask the listener to find a paragraph in a magazine or a newspaper that has information to be recalled.) Using this article, identify who, what, when, where, why, and how. Practice recalling the information. How does the wh-question strategy work for you? In what other situation might you hear information that these questions would help you to remember (e.g., an announcement on the radio for a concert you want to attend)?

How to Dive for Treasures

Reference: McNiff, T. (1981, August 17). Sunken treasure...? A dangerous search of the Andrea Doria. *The Boston Globe*, pp. 1, 16.

Materials

None

Orienting the Listener

In this lesson, you are a diver looking for a treasure. The treasure you want is on the ocean floor. You must listen very carefully, because a mistake may cause you to lose the treasure. Even worse, a mistake may cost you your life.

Additional Memory Strategies: Organization; Counting

A speaker may provide statements that give you a clue to a change in ideas. The directions I'll read to you contain several clues. They help you to know when there is a shift in the topic.

(Point out the introductory statements like, "You must do some research," which introduces paragraph one. Paragraph two is full of transitions to the next two paragraphs [safety and locating the treasure]. Help the listeners identify those statements while listening to the passage a second time.)

The Information (23 Facts)

Before you leave for your adventure, you must do some research. Find out <u>where</u> a ship has gone down. Find out w<u>hat the treasure</u> is, so you will know if making a dive is worth your time and money. Also, find out where the treasure was <u>kept in the shi</u>p. Are diamonds in the office safe? Is gold stored in the hold of the ship?

That is only the beginning. After you have chosen a treasure and know where it is, you must c<u>hoose your equipmen</u>t. You will need equipment to supply you with air and to protect you from the water pressure as you go deeper.

A d<u>iving bel</u>l will help you to get deep into the ocean. Once you are there, you will need special equipment for breathing. You will breathe a mixture of 9<u>0 percent</u> <u>helium</u> and 1<u>0 percent</u> <u>oxygen</u>. That mixture will help to <u>prevent sleepines</u>s and the <u>bends</u>. People get the bends w<u>hen they rise</u> to the surface of the ocean too quickly. It is painful and sometimes deadly. A decompression chamber will help you to prevent the bends. In a decompression chamber, you slowly will experience a change from a great amount of pressure to regular pressure.

You not only need equipment for your safety, you also need equipment to locate the treasure. You will need lights. It is dark down on the ocean bottom. You may need a suction hose to vacuum mud and other things covering parts of the ship. You will need tools to move rusty doors. You will also need ropes and machines to lift the treasure.

After months of work, you may succeed. The safe on the Andrea Doria was found 25 years after the ship sank. The safe was deep in the ship, and the ship was 160 feet under the water.

This was an example of another oral direction that alerted you to the steps and organization of thinking by using the words *first* and *second*. Did you notice them? Were they helpful?

Suggestions for Generalization

Pretend you are a student and a research paper is assigned. Your teacher told you the steps. You heard the teacher saying something like this: "First, choose a topic. Next, go to the library and see what books you can find. Then, as you read, take notes on note cards." Do you remember hearing a teacher say that? Now that you know that counting is a helpful strategy, how can that help you in listening to speakers such as a teacher (e.g., listening for steps, making sure you understand all of the steps, listing the steps in your notes and numbering them, etc.)? How would this strategy be useful in an employment setting?

Making a Movie

References: Thomas, J. (1981, December 4). Inside look at the filming of a thriller. *The Boston Globe*, pp. 37–38.

Schuman, P. (1981, December 5). The making of "Raiders of the Lost Ark." *Public Broadcasting System*, Channel 2, Boston.

Materials

None

Orienting the Listener

You have a job. It is a challenging but exciting job. You are in charge of organizing the supplies for making a movie. The movie is *Raiders of the Lost Ark*. You are going to be responsible for many things. Imagine yourself doing these things. Make connections for the places and for the numbers you hear in the directions I will read.

Additional Memory Strategy: Counting

This would be an interesting job to have. There are a lot of names and numbers to remember, which is challenging. You can organize your responsibilities by counting how many things you actually have to do.

The Information (30 Facts)

Your bosses are <u>George</u> <u>Lucas</u> and <u>Steven</u> <u>Spielberg</u>. Remembering their initials might be helpful here. The filming is going to take place in the <u>Sahara Desert</u> in <u>North Africa</u>. It is very important to organize well, because you will be <u>60 kilometers</u> from the nearest settlement. There are three things you can begin to arrange now. First, you are going to have to arrange for <u>600 extras</u> to play parts in the movie. You can get them from <u>Tunisia</u>. The second thing to get is <u>water</u>. It is very hot in the desert. It will be <u>120 degrees in the shade</u> and <u>130 degrees in the sun</u>, so water will be very important. You will need to get <u>5,000</u> to <u>10,000 gallons of water</u> <u>daily</u>. There is one last thing to arrange for now. There will be a snake scene in the movie. The <u>two main characters</u> in the movie will fall into a <u>pit full of snakes</u>. You will have to find <u>9,000 snakes</u> to put into the pit. Be sure to include some <u>pythons</u> and <u>cobras</u>. Most of the snakes can be small harmless ones. Be sure to get some <u>antivenin serum</u> just in case someone is bitten. When you get that done, <u>report back</u> to the <u>movie director</u>.

Suggestions for Generalization

When you go to a movie that you like, you will want to know the names of the actors so you can watch for them in other movies. We are going to practice remembering names using any strategies you find useful. (Choose a current popular movie with less-well-known actors in it, ones that the participants might be interested in remembering.) It is important to repeat a name a few times to make sure that you can say it correctly. If you can't say it correctly, you probably won't remember it. In addition to saying it, you could write it. What are some other strategies you could use? How can you associate that name with the name of the movie so that you will remember which movie the actor is in?

Microscope

Reference: Microscope. (1980). In *The World Book encyclopedia* (Vol. 13, p. 426). Chicago: World Book Childcraft.

Materials

Diagram of a Microscope (See page 137; duplicate one per participant.)

Orienting the Listener

(Distribute the microscope diagrams to participants.) When you are in science class, you often do experiments. We are going to pretend that you are being taught to use a microscope. After I'm done giving directions, I want you to be able to tell me how to use it. (Or the participants may write down how to use it.) I will give you a few minutes to study the *Diagram of a Microscope* and to remember the names of the parts.

On the nosepiece are three lenses (pause). The whole nosepiece turns so you can use the lenses one at a time. The one that is pointing straight down is the one that is ready to be used. Each lens is a different strength. The low-power lens makes things look a little bigger than they are. The medium-power lens makes things *even* bigger. The high-power lens makes things look *much* bigger.

Additional Memory Strategy: Knowledge Base; Key Words

The steps in using the microscope must be done in the correct order. You can imagine yourself using it, or you can imagine a path or line from one part of the microscope to another as you hear the steps. Then you just need to follow your imaginary path again to remember how to use the microscope.

Whenever you are given something like a diagram, picture, map, graph, or chart, it is helpful to look at it and to learn as much about it as you can. Then when you are listening, you don't have to work so hard at finding things and figuring them out. (Give the participants enough time to review the diagram.)

Look at the parts of the microscope. Some of them will be easy to remember because you can imagine why they were named the way they are (e.g., nosepiece, eyepiece, foot).

The Information (15 Facts)

To begin, you must <u>turn the nosepiece</u> so that you have the <u>low-power lens</u> pointing to the stage. Now turn the <u>coarse-adjustment knob</u> to move the lens a<u>lmost all the way down</u> to the stage. The lens is all set.

Now notice that there is a mirror below the stage. The mirror can reflect light up through the hole in the stage. Look <u>through the eyepiece</u> while you ad<u>just the mirror</u>. Adjust the mirror so that you can see a bright c<u>ircle of light through</u> the eyepiece. Your lens is ready and the light is all set.

Now you are ready for a slide. The flat piece of glass is called a slide. Pretend this particular slide has a tiny animal on it. It is so tiny that you can't see it with the naked eye. Put the <u>slide on the stag</u>e. Hold the slide there by putting the <u>clips</u> on it. The light will shine up through the slide so you can see it well.

Now back to the lens. You need to <u>focus</u> the lens. You do this by <u>raising the lens</u>. Use the c<u>oarse-adjustment knob</u> to do this. You used this knob once before. While you turn the knob, watch the slide through the eyepiece. Turn the knob until the animal is in focus. D<u>on't lower the len</u>s. You could break the slide and the lens.

The last step is to turn the nosepiece to a <u>higher-powered len</u>s. It will make the animal look larger. You will be able to see more details this way. Use the <u>fine adjustmen</u>t knob to focus.

Suggestions for Generalization

You may want to recall the names of characters in a book. (The following example is for students.) If you are required to read the book and are being tested on it, you will want to remember each character's name and at least one key word to identify who that person is. (The following example is for adults.) You may enjoy discussing books with a book club or just with friends. For practice, bring in your favorite book and tell us how you would associate the names with associations for the characters or use the characters of a favorite TV show.

Diagram of a Microscope

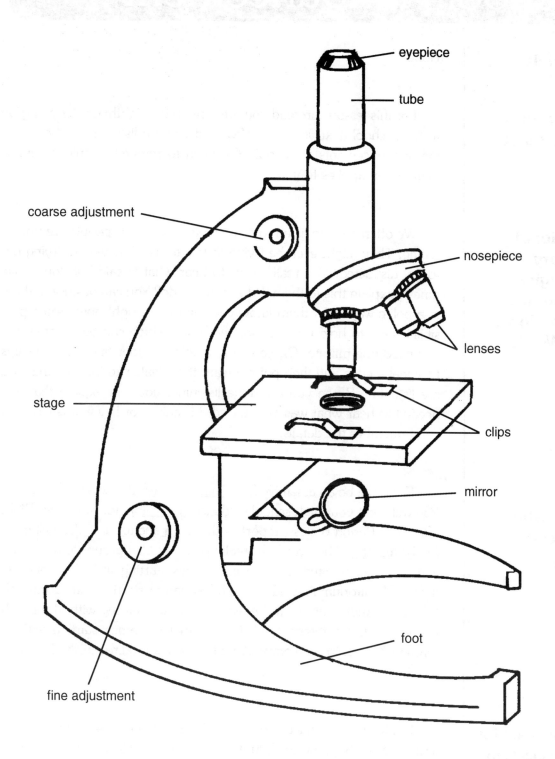

eyepiece

tube

coarse adjustment

nosepiece

lenses

stage

clips

mirror

fine adjustment

foot

© 1997 Thinking Publications. Duplication permitted for educational use only.

School Announcement

Materials

None

Orienting the Listener

For this lesson, pretend you are a ninth (or eighth) grader going on to high school next year. It is May, and you are listening to the morning announcements at school. You need to remember only the information that applies to you.

Additional Memory Strategies: Eliminating Distractions; Key Words

We often have to listen to something when other people are not listening. They might even be trying to talk to us while we are trying not to get distracted. You really want to hear what is said but don't have time to explain this to them. What can you do? You can gesture to them in a polite way to let them know you can't listen right now. Some possibilities are to hold up your pointer finger, which can be a signal that you need one minute. Or, you can politely put your finger to your lips to signal silence and then point toward the speaker to indicate that you are listening. When you are done listening, you can explain that you needed to hear what was announced. Listening for key words will help you remember the details.

The Information (7 Facts)

There will be an assembly for all ninth graders during seventh period. You will meet your high school guidance counselors for next year. Right after your Period 6 class, report to the main auditorium. You will meet for 10 minutes. Then you will break up into smaller groups to meet with your counselors. Students with last names starting with A through C meet in Auditorium A; students with last names starting with D through L meet in Auditorium B; those with last names starting with M through P meet in the cafeteria; and those with last names starting with Q through Z meet in the library. (One location is required in the listener's recall.)

Suggestions for Generalization

Think of other places you might hear announcements (e.g., in an airport, in a shopping mall, in a discount store). How could you eliminate distractions in these settings? What key words might you expect to hear in each setting?

Homework Assignments

Materials

None

Orienting the Listener

I'm going to give you information for different kinds of assignments. Listen for key words to help you remember. Ask me to repeat the information if necessary.

Additional Memory Strategies: Asking for Repetition; Key Words

On homework assignments, there is no room for error. You must get it right or you won't get credit. If you do the even numbers in math and the odd numbers were assigned, it will affect your grade. If your report is due on Friday *this* week and you think it is Friday of *next* week, you could lose important time and could also lose some points. It is important to ask for a repetition when in doubt or to double-check the assignment with a friend. Listening for key words also will help you remember.

I. The Information (13 Facts)

This is a homework assignment for a big paper that's due. A large part of your grade will be based on the paper. Listen carefully: For the paper you are <u>going to write</u>, choose a <u>topic</u> and check out <u>four</u> <u>books</u> from the library by <u>next Tuesday</u>. Begin taking notes from the books. Write the notes on note cards. Bring in <u>30</u> <u>note card</u>s by the <u>following Tuesday</u>. Then your <u>outline</u> is due that <u>Friday</u>. Have a <u>rough draft</u> of the paper ready in <u>three</u> <u>weeks</u>.

II. The Information (8 Facts)

This is a regular homework assignment. Listen carefully: We're beginning <u>Chapter</u> <u>10</u> <u>tomorrow</u>. <u>Tonight</u> read pages <u>201</u> to <u>205</u>. Write answers to <u>questions</u> <u>1–4</u> at the end of the chapter.

III. The Information (11 Facts)

You have a big test coming up. The teacher is describing it: The end-of-term test will cover <u>Chapters</u> <u>13–17</u>. I suggest that you concentrate on the <u>study sheet</u> that I've given you. There will be some <u>matching</u>, some <u>true-false</u>, and o<u>ne diagram</u> to label. The test is <u>Friday</u>. We will <u>review</u> for the test on <u>Thursday</u>. Bring in any <u>questions</u> you have on Thursday. If you study about h<u>alf an hour each night</u>, you'll do okay.

IV. The Information (13 Facts)

These are comments a teacher is making about a test: There will be a test on <u>Tuesday</u>. It will cover the <u>causes of the Civil War</u>, which should be in your <u>notes</u> from last week. Also, you will be responsible for reading and knowing the information in <u>Chapter 10</u>, pages <u>214</u>–<u>222</u>. The <u>questions</u> at the end of the chapter are a good review for the test. It will be an <u>open-book</u> test. There will be <u>20</u> <u>fill-in-the-blank questions</u> and <u>2 essay question</u>s.

Suggestions for Generalization

Pretend you are a classroom teacher. Write down five different assignments you will give to your students this week. Decide if you will allow students to ask questions. Read the assignments to the participants in this group. Discuss the strategies listeners used to remember the assignments.

Job Directions

Materials

None

Orienting the Listener

I'm going to read directions that you might hear at a job.

Additional Memory Strategy: Kinesthetic Imagery

When directions involve moving around, one strategy that can be helpful is to imagine yourself doing what is asked so that you have those images to replay like a video in your mind.

I. The Information (14 Facts)

These directions might be given to a person employed in a maintenance department: Sweep the rooms on the <u>first floor first</u>, because there is a <u>meeting</u> there tonight at <u>7:00</u>. In Room <u>112</u>, put <u>two long tables side by side</u> so they <u>form a square</u> (provide a gesture). Arrange <u>10 chairs</u> around the tables. There is a <u>game in the gym</u> that will be over at about <u>5:00</u>. Make certain that <u>everyone is out</u>. <u>Sweep</u> up, then <u>lock</u> the gym doors.

II. The Information (10 Facts)

These directions might be given to a person employed in a supermarket: First, <u>sweep up the broken bottle</u> in <u>Aisle 6</u>. Then, bring the <u>shopping carts</u> in from the <u>parking lot</u>. Next, help <u>bag groceries</u> at any checkout that seems to be <u>slow</u>. <u>After the store closes</u>, <u>sweep</u> out the <u>back</u> room.

III. The Information (13 Facts)

These directions might be given to a receptionist employed at a doctor's office: <u>Call Mr. Walker</u> and tell him <u>Mrs. Walker</u> is going to the <u>hospital</u> <u>right away</u>. Try him at <u>work first</u>, then <u>at home</u>. Tell him to meet me in the <u>admitting room</u> at <u>General Hospital</u>. <u>Call the hospital</u> and tell them we will be there in <u>10 minutes</u>.

Suggestions for Generalization

Think of other situations in which directions are given to you. Discuss whether a kinesthetic imagery strategy would help you to recall the directions. If not, what other strategies might work?

Appendices

Appendices

Checklist of Informal Indicators of Memory— Version 1

Name _____

Date _____ Class_____

	YES	NO

Academic Performance in Class

On tests, recalls facts such as names and dates as easily as concepts . . . . ☐   ☐

Recalls meanings of words on vocabulary tests . . . . ☐   ☐

Recalls information during discussions . . . . ☐   ☐

Recalls oral directions given in class . . . . ☐   ☐

Follows oral directions in correct sequence . . . . ☐   ☐

Completes assignments (using the correct pages, preparing the
    correct length, addressing the correct topic, etc.) . . . . ☐   ☐

Takes notes with important information included . . . . ☐   ☐

Receives consistent scores on classwork, homework, and tests . . . . ☐   ☐

Receives scores on standardized achievement tests that are consistent
    with class grades . . . . ☐   ☐

Behavioral Traits in Classroom

Experiences frustration when required to recall information . . . . ☐   ☐

Produces inconsistent work, reflecting confusion due to poor memory or recall . . ☐   ☐

Avoids participating in class; is very quiet . . . . ☐   ☐

Lies or cheats to cover up errors . . . . ☐   ☐

Has low motivation . . . . ☐   ☐

Prefers reading over listening tasks . . . . ☐   ☐

© 1997 Thinking Publications. Duplication permitted for educational use only.

Checklist of Informal Indicators of Memory—
Version 2

Name _____ Date _____

	YES	NO

Performance at Home/on the Job

Recalls facts such as names and dates as easily as concepts . . . . ☐   ☐

Recalls meanings of words . . . . ☐   ☐

Recalls information during discussions . . . . ☐   ☐

Recalls oral directions given at home and/or work . . . . ☐   ☐

Follows oral directions in correct sequence . . . . ☐   ☐

Completes tasks correctly following oral directions . . . . ☐   ☐

Takes notes when needed (e.g., phone messages) . . . . ☐   ☐

Demonstrates consistent listening and recall skills . . . . ☐   ☐

Behavioral Traits

Experiences frustration when required to recall information . . . . ☐   ☐

Produces inconsistent work, reflecting confusion due to poor memory or recall . . ☐   ☐

Avoids participating; is very quiet . . . . ☐   ☐

Lies or cheats to cover up errors . . . . ☐   ☐

Has low motivation . . . . ☐   ☐

Prefers reading over listening tasks . . . . ☐   ☐

 © 1997 Thinking Publications. Duplication permitted for educational use only.

Progress Sheet

Name _____   Date _____

Date	Presentation	Results	Comments

© 1997 Thinking Publications. Duplication permitted for educational use only.

Steps to Success

Name _____   Date _____

Oral Directions

Date begun: _____

Date completed: _____

Articles

Date begun: _____

Date completed: _____

Paragraphs

Date begun: _____

Date completed: _____

Words

Date begun: _____

Date completed: _____

© 1997 Thinking Publications. Duplication permitted for educational use only.

Story 1, Card 1

Words   *Verbal Association*

ship   A branch is sailing a
branch   ship.

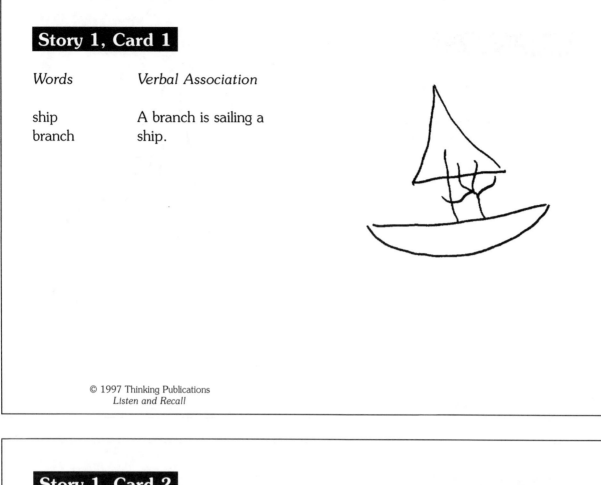

© 1997 Thinking Publications
Listen and Recall

Story 1, Card 2

Words   *Verbal Association*

wrench   She hits a wrench and it
                makes a hole in the ship.

© 1997 Thinking Publications
Listen and Recall

© 1997 Thinking Publications. Duplication permitted for educational use only.

Story 1, Card 3

Words	Verbal Association
web	She patches the hole with a web.

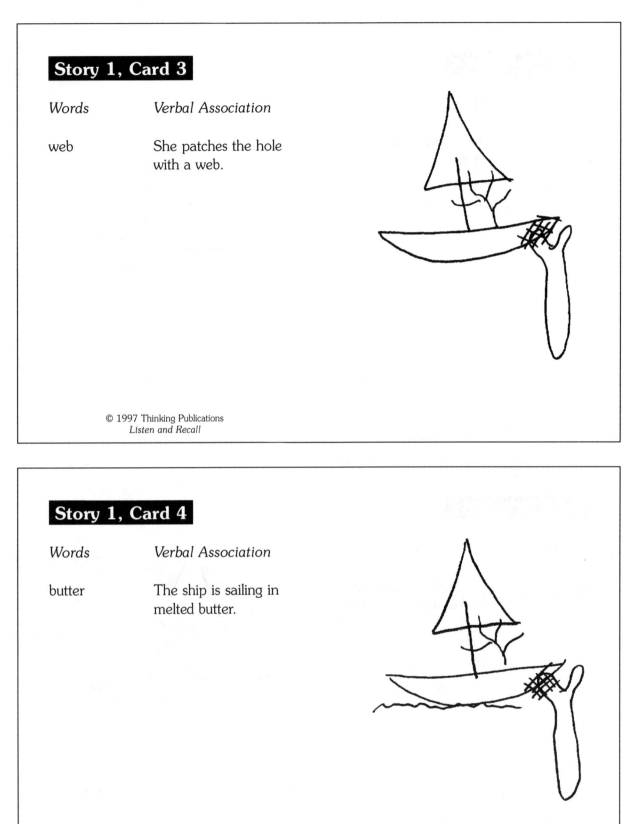

© 1997 Thinking Publications
Listen and Recall

Story 1, Card 4

Words	Verbal Association
butter	The ship is sailing in melted butter.

© 1997 Thinking Publications
Listen and Recall

 © 1997 Thinking Publications. Duplication permitted for educational use only.

Story 1, Card 5

Words	*Verbal Association*
piano	A piano is a pirate that robs the ship.

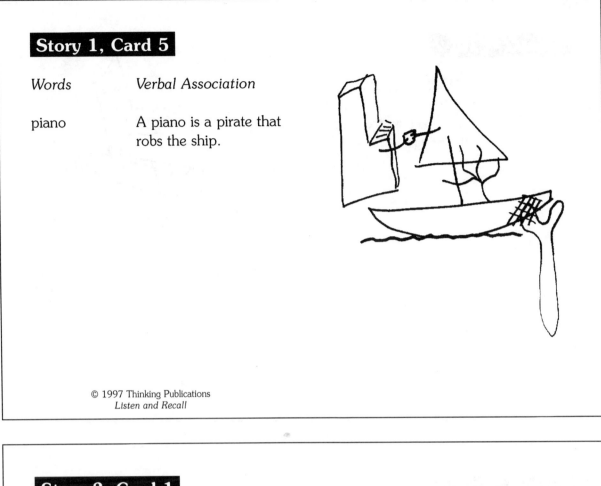

© 1997 Thinking Publications
Listen and Recall

Story 2, Card 1

Words	*Verbal Association*
mountain bandage	There was a mountain with two peaks. A giant bandage was used as a bridge between the two peaks.

© 1997 Thinking Publications
Listen and Recall

© 1997 Thinking Publications. Duplication permitted for educational use only.

Story 2, Card 2

Words	Verbal Association
blanket	A blanket started across the bridge.

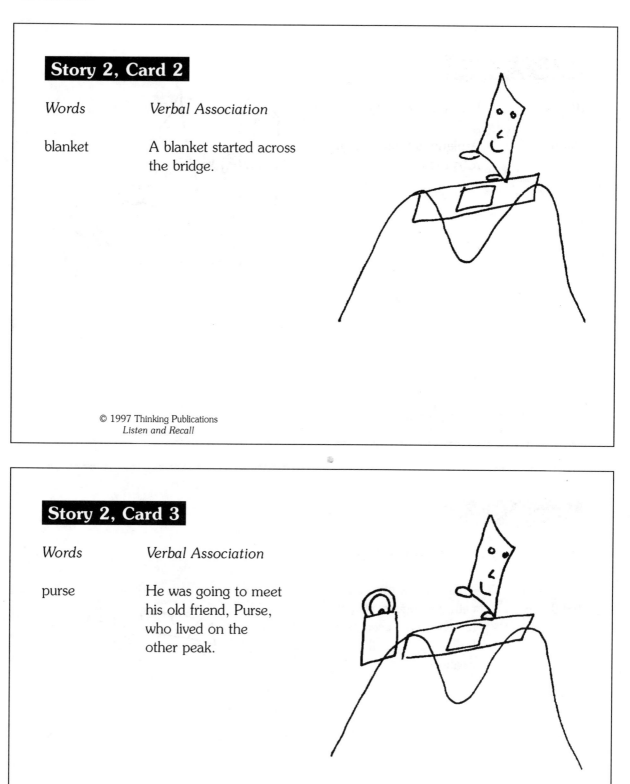

© 1997 Thinking Publications
Listen and Recall

Story 2, Card 3

Words	Verbal Association
purse	He was going to meet his old friend, Purse, who lived on the other peak.

© 1997 Thinking Publications
Listen and Recall

©1997 Thinking Publications. Duplication permitted for educational use only.

Story 2, Card 4

Words

smoke

Verbal Association

The purse had a fire
going, and the smoke
got in the blanket's eyes.

© 1997 Thinking Publications
Listen and Recall

Story 2, Card 5

Words

snow

Verbal Association

The blanket fell into
some snow.

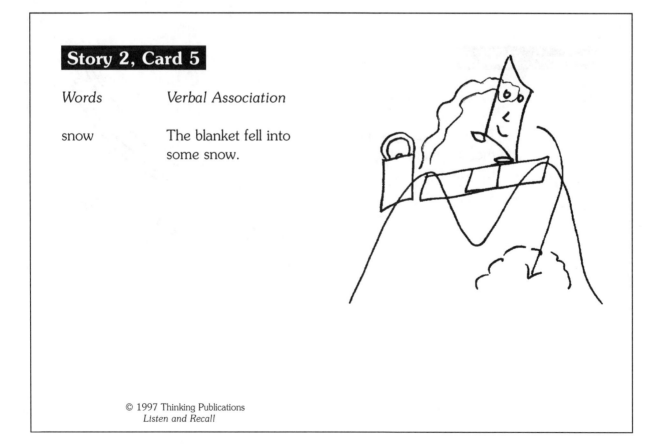

© 1997 Thinking Publications
Listen and Recall

Story 3, Card 1

Words	Verbal Association
wig triangle	Two wigs were using a triangle to play catch.

© 1997 Thinking Publications
Listen and Recall

Story 3, Card 2

Words	Verbal Association
skis	A pair of skis flew out of the sky and grabbed the triangle.

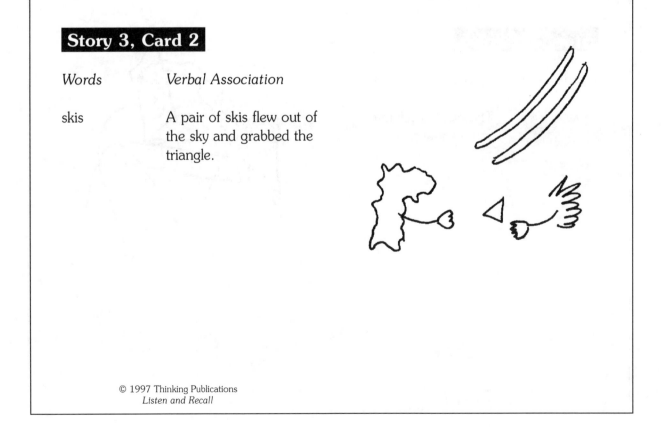

© 1997 Thinking Publications
Listen and Recall

 © 1997 Thinking Publications. Duplication permitted for educational use only.

Story 3, Card 3

Words   *Verbal Association*

stocking   One of the wigs had a
loose stocking. She
tripped over it.

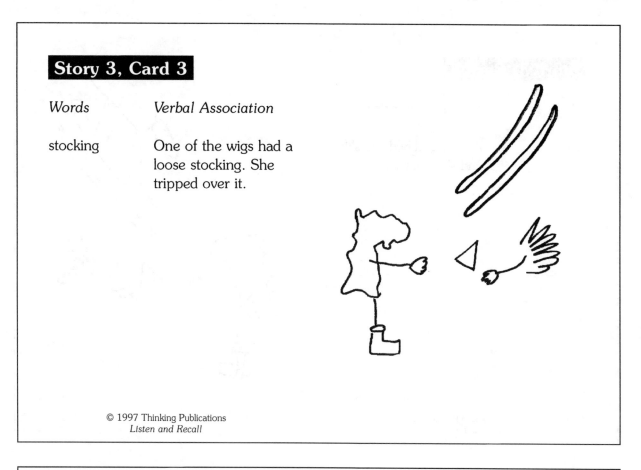

© 1997 Thinking Publications
Listen and Recall

Story 3, Card 4

Words   *Verbal Association*

belt   She used a belt to hold
up the stocking.

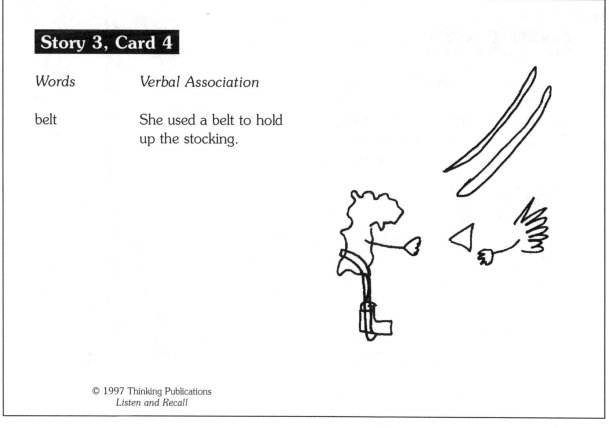

© 1997 Thinking Publications
Listen and Recall

© 1997 Thinking Publications. Duplication permitted for educational use only.

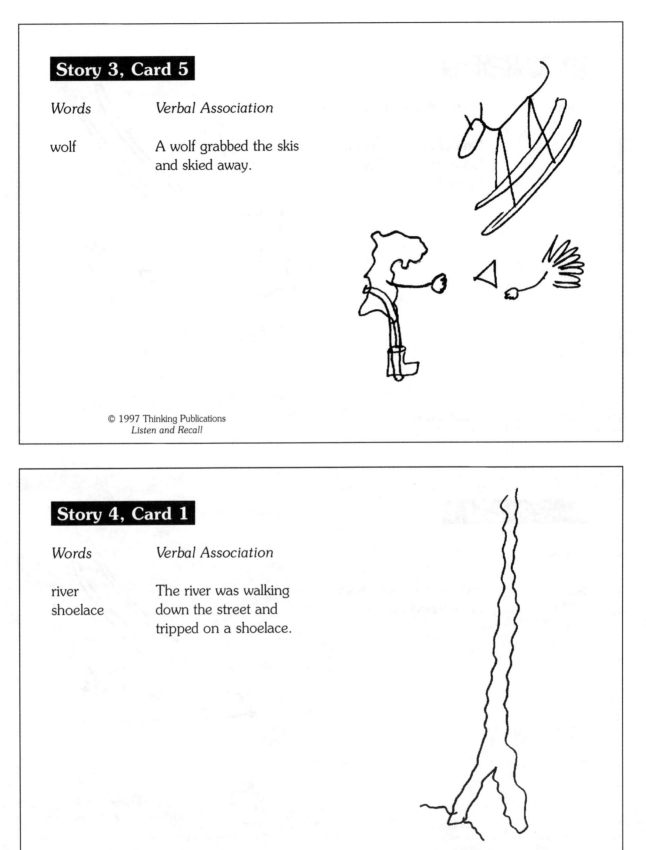

Story 3, Card 5

Words	Verbal Association
wolf	A wolf grabbed the skis and skied away.

© 1997 Thinking Publications
Listen and Recall

Story 4, Card 1

Words	Verbal Association
river	The river was walking
shoelace	down the street and
	tripped on a shoelace.

© 1997 Thinking Publications
Listen and Recall

© 1997 Thinking Publications. Duplication permitted for educational use only.

Story 4, Card 2

Words   *Verbal Association*

leg   The river fell and hurt its leg.

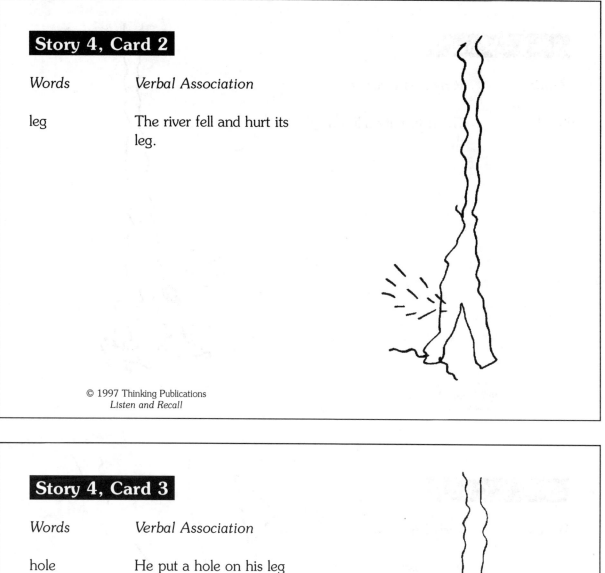

© 1997 Thinking Publications
Listen and Recall

Story 4, Card 3

Words   *Verbal Association*

hole   He put a hole on his leg to stop the bleeding.

© 1997 Thinking Publications
Listen and Recall

© 1997 Thinking Publications. Duplication permitted for educational use only.

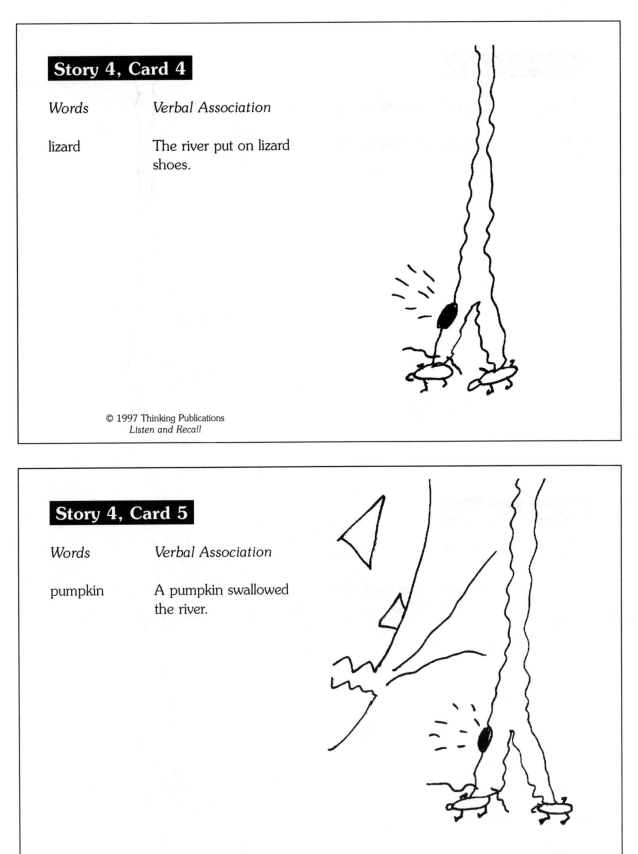

Story 4, Card 4

Words   *Verbal Association*

lizard   The river put on lizard shoes.

© 1997 Thinking Publications
Listen and Recall

Story 4, Card 5

Words   *Verbal Association*

pumpkin   A pumpkin swallowed the river.

© 1997 Thinking Publications
Listen and Recall

  © 1997 Thinking Publications. Duplication permitted for educational use only.

Story 5, Card 1

Words   *Verbal Association*

penguin   There's a giant salt
salt shaker   shaker filled with
                        penguins.

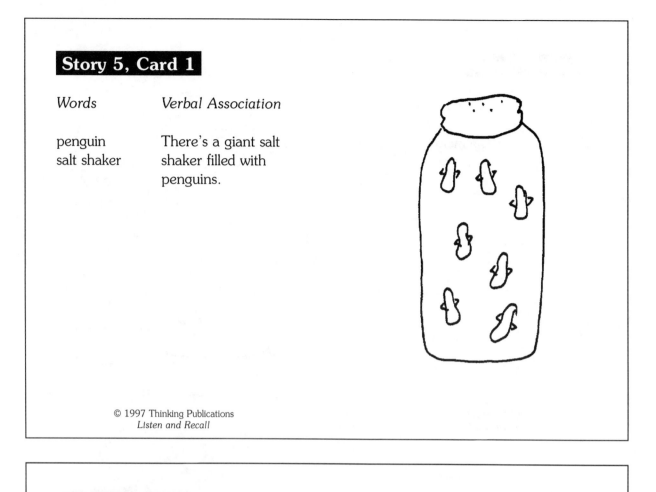

© 1997 Thinking Publications
Listen and Recall

Story 5, Card 2

Words   *Verbal Association*

melon   A melon flies down to
                        see them.

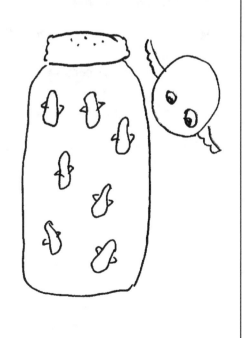

© 1997 Thinking Publications
Listen and Recall

© 1997 Thinking Publications. Duplication permitted for educational use only.

Story 5, Card 3

Words	Verbal Association
pillow	The melon falls on a pillow.

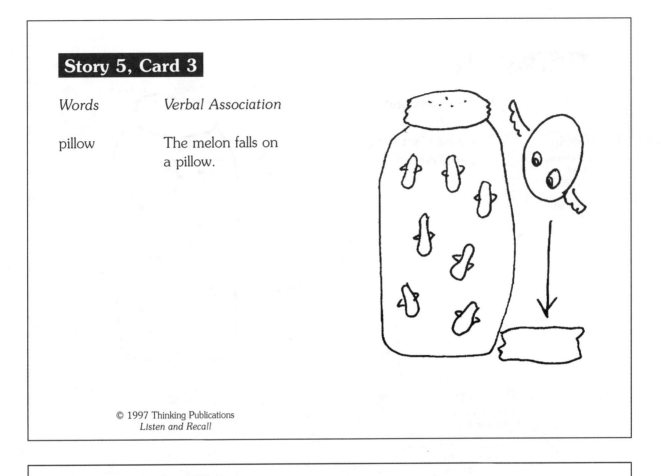

© 1997 Thinking Publications
Listen and Recall

Story 5, Card 4

Words	Verbal Association
camera	A camera opens the salt shaker.

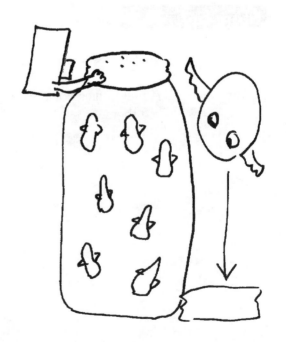

© 1997 Thinking Publications
Listen and Recall

 © 1997 Thinking Publications. Duplication permitted for educational use only.

Story 5, Card 5

Words | *Verbal Association*

beehive | All of the penguins fly over to a beehive and hide in it.

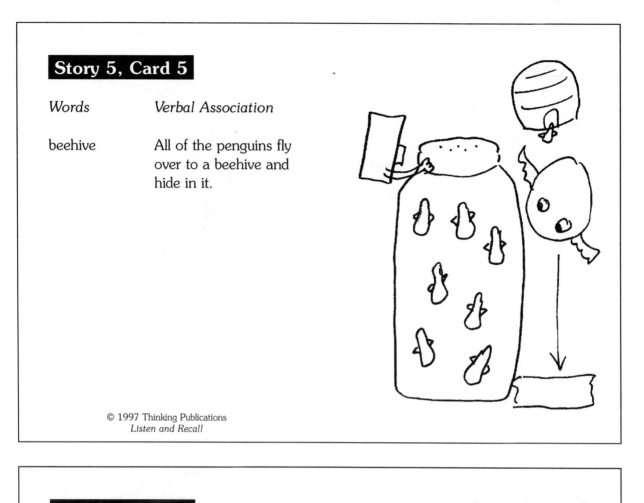

© 1997 Thinking Publications
Listen and Recall

Story 6, Card 1

Words | *Verbal Association*

horseshoe | A bug was tickling
bug | a horseshoe.

© 1997 Thinking Publications
Listen and Recall

© 1997 Thinking Publications. Duplication permitted for educational use only.

Story 6, Card 2

Words	Verbal Association
lock	The horseshoe locked the bug's feet together.

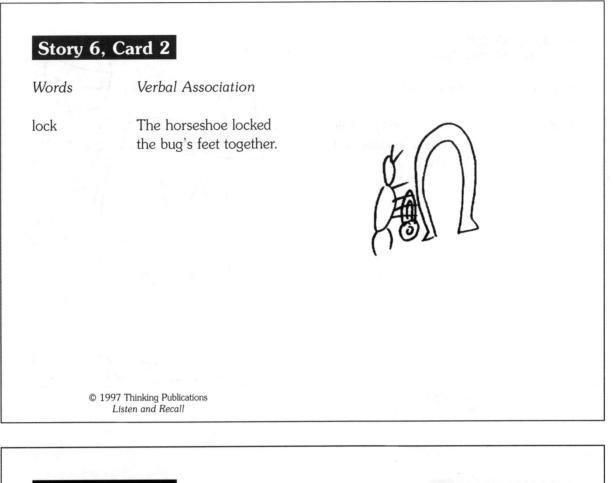

© 1997 Thinking Publications
Listen and Recall

Story 6, Card 3

Words	Verbal Association
whale	The horseshoe leaped on a whale's back and galloped away.

© 1997 Thinking Publications
Listen and Recall

© 1997 Thinking Publications. Duplication permitted for educational use only.

Story 6, Card 4

Words | Verbal Association

seed | The horseshoe dropped seeds onto the ground.

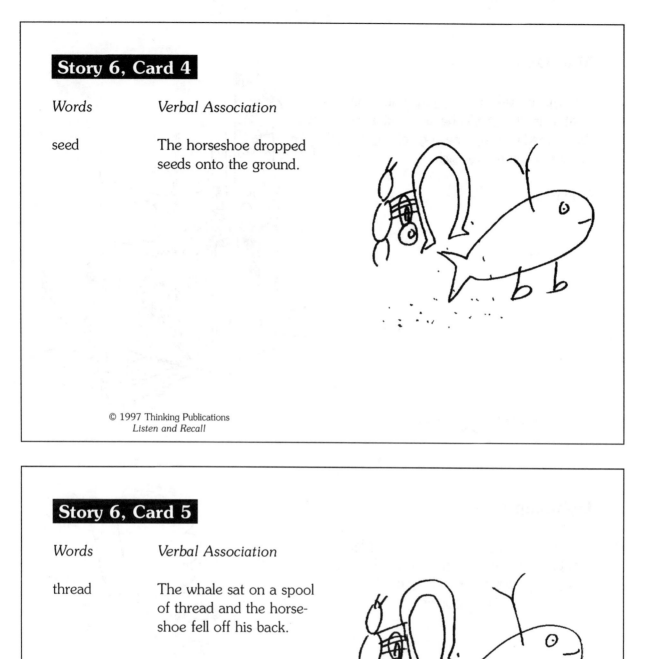

© 1997 Thinking Publications
Listen and Recall

Story 6, Card 5

Words | Verbal Association

thread | The whale sat on a spool of thread and the horse-shoe fell off his back.

© 1997 Thinking Publications
Listen and Recall

© 1997 Thinking Publications. Duplication permitted for educational use only.

Mail Dog

<u>Jim</u> <u>Stacy</u> was a <u>postmaster</u> in <u>Calico</u>, <u>California</u>. In <u>1883</u>, he adopted a stray dog named <u>Dorsey</u>. The <u>dog</u> <u>delivered</u> <u>mail</u> for him when he was <u>sick</u>.

(10 facts)

1   © 1997 Thinking Publications
Listen and Recall

Lightning Healed

<u>Edwin</u> <u>E</u>. <u>Robinson</u> of <u>Falmouth</u>, <u>Maine</u>, was <u>blind</u> and <u>deaf</u> for <u>nine</u> <u>years</u>. In <u>June</u> of <u>1980</u> he was hit by <u>lightning</u>. He could suddenly <u>see</u> and <u>hear</u> <u>again</u>.

(14 facts)

2   © 1997 Thinking Publications
Listen and Recall

            © 1997 Thinking Publications. Duplication permitted for educational use only.

First Photo in the United States

The <u>first</u> <u>photo</u> in the <u>United States</u> required <u>six</u> <u>minutes</u> of <u>sunlight</u> exposure. It was <u>taken by</u> <u>Dr.</u> <u>John</u> <u>William</u> <u>Draper</u> in the <u>summer</u> of <u>1840</u>. He took a picture of his <u>sister</u>, <u>Dorothy</u>.

(15 facts)

3   © 1997 Thinking Publications
Listen and Recall

Trash in New York City

Each year <u>New York City</u> has enough <u>trash</u> to <u>fill</u> a <u>15-square-block</u> area up to <u>20</u> <u>stories high</u>, according to <u>Sherry</u> <u>Koehler</u>, a <u>guide</u> at the <u>Staten Island</u> <u>dump</u>.

(12 facts)

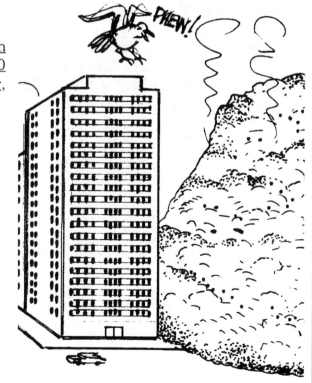

4   © 1997 Thinking Publications
Listen and Recall

© 1997 Thinking Publications. Duplication permitted for educational use only.

First "First Lady"

The <u>first</u> <u>woman</u> to live in the <u>White House</u> was <u>Abigail</u> <u>Adams</u>, the <u>wife</u> of <u>President</u> <u>John</u> <u>Adams</u>. They <u>moved in</u> in <u>1800</u>. The White House was <u>not finished</u>, so she had no place to <u>hang</u> her <u>laundry</u> to dry. She hung it in the <u>East</u> <u>Room</u>.

(16 facts)

© 1997 Thinking Publications
Listen and Recall

Largest Bird

A <u>skeleton</u> of the <u>largest bird</u> that ever lived was found in <u>Argentina</u>. It weighed <u>175</u> <u>pounds</u>, was <u>30</u> <u>feet long</u>, and had a <u>20-foot</u> <u>wing span</u>.

(10 facts)

© 1997 Thinking Publications
Listen and Recall

© 1997 Thinking Publications. Duplication permitted for educational use only.

Johnny Appleseed

Johnny Appleseed's real name was John Chapman. He was born about 1775. He wandered the frontier of Ohio and Indiana. He sold apple seeds and little trees. He was also a messenger in the War of 1812.

(16 facts)

7

© 1997 Thinking Publications
Listen and Recall

Large Eggs

The largest eggs ever laid were more than 12 inches long and 9 inches wide. The bird that laid the eggs was called an Aepyornis (pronounced "ee-pih-or-nis"). It is now extinct. It was 10 feet tall and lived in Madagascar.

(10 facts)

8

© 1997 Thinking Publications
Listen and Recall

© 1997 Thinking Publications. Duplication permitted for educational use only.

First Windshield Wiper

<u>Mary</u> <u>Anderson</u> <u>invented</u> a <u>hand-operated</u> <u>windshield wiper</u> in <u>1902</u>. She obtained a <u>17-year</u> <u>patent</u> on it. By <u>1916</u>, <u>mechanical</u> <u>wiper</u>s were standard <u>equipment</u> on <u>American car</u>s.

(13 facts)

© 1997 Thinking Publications
Listen and Recall

9

Baby Pandas

A <u>Panda</u> named <u>Shao-Shao</u> gave <u>birth</u> to <u>twins</u> on <u>September</u> <u>4</u>, <u>1982</u>, in <u>Madrid</u>, <u>Spain</u>. The <u>mother</u> weighed <u>200</u> <u>pounds</u>. The <u>twins</u> weighed <u>2</u> <u>ounces</u> and <u>3</u> <u>ounces</u>.

(17 facts)

© 1997 Thinking Publications
Listen and Recall

10

 © 1997 Thinking Publications. Duplication permitted for educational use only.

Parachuting Record

<u>Bruce</u> <u>MacLaughlin</u> of <u>Easton</u>, <u>Massachusetts</u>, <u>parachuted</u> from an airplane <u>235</u> times in <u>22</u> <u>hours</u> on <u>September</u> <u>18</u>, <u>1981</u>. He set a new <u>record</u>. He used the <u>Taunton</u> <u>Municipal</u> <u>Airport</u>.

(15 facts)

11 © 1997 Thinking Publications
Listen and Recall

Ice Age Drawings

In <u>1879</u>, a <u>9-year</u>-old girl was <u>exploring</u> <u>Altamira</u> <u>Cave</u> in <u>Spain</u>. She discovered <u>drawings</u> on the wall. The girl, <u>Maria</u>, had found <u>Ice</u> <u>Age</u> drawings that were <u>16,000</u> <u>years</u> old.

(13 facts)

12 © 1997 Thinking Publications
Listen and Recall

© 1997 Thinking Publications. Duplication permitted for educational use only.

The Oldest Dental Filling

A <u>man</u> had a <u>cavity</u> and he wanted it fixed. He lived <u>2,200</u> <u>years</u> ago. People living long ago believed <u>tooth worm</u>s caused cavities, so they stuck a <u>bronze wire</u> <u>into the</u> <u>man's tooth</u>. This must have been very <u>painful</u>. People believed in tooth worms <u>until</u> <u>300</u> <u>years</u> ago.

(11 facts)

13   © 1997 Thinking Publications
Listen and Recall

Youngest College Graduate

<u>Jay</u> <u>Luo</u> <u>went</u> to <u>college</u> when he was <u>9</u> <u>years</u> old. He <u>graduated</u> from <u>Boise</u> <u>State</u> <u>College</u> in <u>Idaho</u> in <u>May</u> <u>1982</u>, at the age of <u>12</u>. His <u>parents</u> came <u>to</u> the <u>United</u> <u>State</u>s from <u>Taiwan</u>.

(18 facts)

14   © 1997 Thinking Publications
Listen and Recall

 © 1997 Thinking Publications. Duplication permitted for educational use only.

Incredible Swim

At age <u>70</u>, <u>Jack</u> <u>LaLanne</u> was able to <u>swim</u> a <u>mile</u> <u>towing</u> <u>70</u> <u>boats</u> <u>full of people</u>. His <u>hands</u> and <u>feet</u> were <u>tied</u>. This happened on <u>November</u> <u>20</u>, <u>1984</u>, in <u>Long Beach Harbor</u>, <u>California</u>.

(18 facts)

15 © 1997 Thinking Publications
Listen and Recall

Ocean Crossing

<u>Bill</u> <u>Dunlop</u> of <u>Mechanic Falls</u>, <u>Maine</u>, <u>crossed</u> the <u>Atlantic Ocean</u> in a <u>sailboat</u> that was <u>9</u> <u>feet</u>, <u>1</u> <u>inch long</u>. He sailed on <u>June</u> <u>13</u>, <u>1982</u>. The trip took <u>2</u> <u>months</u> and <u>15</u> <u>days</u>.

(19 facts)

16 © 1997 Thinking Publications
Listen and Recall

© 1997 Thinking Publications. Duplication permitted for educational use only.

Fire Eater

<u>Spira</u> <u>Lloyd</u> of <u>Adelaide</u>, <u>Australia</u>, <u>swal-</u><u>lowed</u> <u>fir</u>e from <u>5,658</u> <u>burning</u> <u>stick</u>s in <u>2</u> <u>hours</u> on a <u>Friday</u> in <u>August</u> <u>1982</u>.

(12 facts)

© 1997 Thinking Publications
Listen and Recall

Discovering a Comet

<u>Maria</u> <u>Mitchell</u> grew up on <u>N</u><u>antucket</u> <u>Island</u> off <u>Massachusetts</u>. She <u>taught her-</u><u>self</u> to be an expert <u>astronomer</u>. On <u>October</u> <u>1</u>, <u>1947</u>, at <u>10:30 p.</u>m., she <u>dis-</u><u>covered</u> a <u>comet</u> that <u>no one else</u> in the world had seen.

(13 facts)

© 1997 Thinking Publications
Listen and Recall

 © 1997 Thinking Publications. Duplication permitted for educational use only.

A Weighty May

T. J. Albert Jackson from Tampa, Florida, was 6 feet, 4 inches tall. He weighed 872 pounds when he was 42 years old. When he caught an airplane in Miami, he was wheeled in on a baggage cart.

(17 facts)

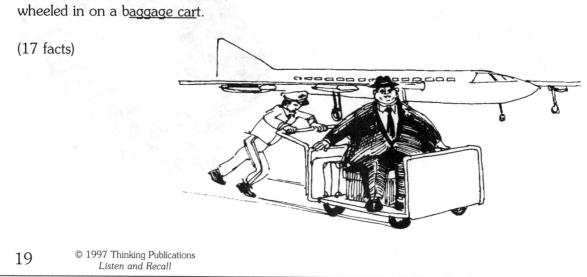

19   © 1997 Thinking Publications
Listen and Recall

Elephant Snorkel

Three days of rain caused severe flooding at the Frank Buck Zoo in Gainesville, Texas. A 13-year-old elephant named Gerry was trapped by a fallen tree. She saved her life by using her trunk as a snorkel. This was in October of 1981.

(20 facts)

20   © 1997 Thinking Publications
Listen and Recall

© 1997 Thinking Publications. Duplication permitted for educational use only.

Secret Notes

<u>Leonardo</u> <u>da Vinci</u> was an <u>inventor</u>, <u>musician</u>, <u>artist</u>, and <u>scientist</u>. He was <u>born</u> in <u>Vinci</u>, <u>Italy</u>, in <u>1452</u>. He <u>wrote</u> more than <u>7,000</u> <u>pages</u> of notes. Most of his notes were <u>written</u> <u>backwards</u>. He would <u>read</u> them with a <u>mirror</u>.

(16 facts)

© 1997 Thinking Publications
Listen and Recall

Power Lifting

<u>Audrey</u> <u>Nobbe</u> is a <u>72-year</u>-old <u>great-grandmother</u> from <u>Woodlawn</u>, <u>Illinois</u>. She has been practicing the sport of <u>power lifting</u> for <u>3</u> <u>years</u>. She has <u>4</u> <u>world records</u> in the <u>over-50</u> age group. She <u>deadlifted</u> <u>215</u> <u>pounds.</u> She is <u>4</u> <u>feet</u> <u>10</u> <u>inches tall</u> and weighs <u>120</u> <u>pounds.</u>

(22 facts)

© 1997 Thinking Publications
Listen and Recall

 © 1997 Thinking Publications. Duplication permitted for educational use only.

Rhino Elected

<u>People</u> who lived in <u>Sao</u> <u>Paulo</u>, <u>Brazil</u>, were <u>upset</u> with their <u>city council</u> members, so they <u>elected</u> a <u>rhino</u>, <u>Cacareco</u>, as a protest. The rhino received <u>100,000 votes</u> on <u>October</u> <u>4</u>, <u>1959</u>. She received m<u>ore vot</u>es than any of the human candidates.

(15 facts)

© 1997 Thinking Publications
Listen and Recall

Unexpected Strength

In <u>October</u> of <u>1980</u>, a <u>5-year</u>-old child named <u>Philip</u> <u>Toth</u> was <u>trapped</u> under an <u>iron pip</u>e. <u>Arnold</u> <u>Lemerand</u> of <u>Southgate</u>, <u>Michigan</u>, who was <u>56</u>, <u>lifted</u> the pipe. The <u>pipe</u> weighed <u>1,800</u> <u>pounds</u>, <u>too heavy</u> for <u>s</u>everal me<u>n</u> to lift.

(19 facts)

© 1997 Thinking Publications
Listen and Recall

© 1997 Thinking Publications. Duplication permitted for educational use only.

Musical Minutes

<u>Luciano</u> <u>Pavarotti</u>, an o<u>pera star</u>, was <u>paid</u> $227 (<u>two-hundred twenty-seven</u> <u>dollars</u>) <u>per minute</u> (about $27,300 [<u>twenty-seven</u> <u>thousand three hundred</u> <u>dollars</u>] for a <u>two-hour</u> <u>concert</u>) in <u>Manchester</u>, <u>England</u>, on <u>October</u> <u>26</u>, <u>1981</u>.

(17 facts)

© 1997 Thinking Publications
Listen and Recall

25

Young Chess Player

On <u>August</u> <u>24</u>, <u>1981</u>, <u>9</u> <u>year</u>-old <u>Sabrena</u> <u>Needham</u> played in a w<u>orld chess contes</u>t in <u>London</u>. She <u>played</u> for <u>20</u> <u>minutes</u> <u>against</u> <u>Russian</u> <u>Grandmaster</u> <u>Vassily</u> <u>Smylov</u>.

(17 facts)

© 1997 Thinking Publications
Listen and Recall

26

© 1997 Thinking Publications. Duplication permitted for educational use only.

Deadly Mushroom

There are about <u>38,000</u> <u>kinds of mush-</u><u>rooms</u>. <u>Aleksey</u> <u>Mikhailovich</u> (<u>Czar</u> <u>Alexis</u>) of <u>Russia</u>, <u>born</u> in <u>1645</u>, <u>died</u> in <u>1676</u> after he <u>ate</u> the deadly <u>Amanita</u> mushroom.

(13 facts)

27   © 1997 Thinking Publications
      Listen and Recall

An Ancient Food

A <u>food</u> <u>grown</u> <u>by</u> the <u>Aztec</u> <u>Indians</u> of <u>Mexico</u> was <u>used</u> in <u>ceremonies</u>. The plant is called <u>amaranth</u>. <u>Hernando</u> <u>Cortez</u> of <u>Spain</u> wanted to <u>get rid</u> of the <u>Aztec cul-</u><u>ture</u>. In <u>1519</u>, <u>anyone</u> <u>growing the plant</u> would <u>lose</u> his <u>hand</u>.

(18 facts)

28   © 1997 Thinking Publications
      Listen and Recall

© 1997 Thinking Publications. Duplication permitted for educational use only.

Great White Shark

Japanese fisherman caught a great white shark in June of 1981. It weighed 3,939 pounds and was 17 feet long. It was caught in the East China Sea near Okinawa.

(14 facts)

29   © 1997 Thinking Publications
Listen and Recall

Hot Spot

The hottest temperature recorded in the world was 136 degrees Fahrenheit (or 58 degrees centigrade) in the shade. It was in Aziza, Libya, which is in the Sahara Desert. The Sahara is about 3,500,000 square miles (about the size of the United States).

(13 facts)

30   © 1997 Thinking Publications
Listen and Recall

    © 1997 Thinking Publications. Duplication permitted for educational use only.

Viking Baby

There is some evidence that <u>Vikings</u> from <u>Norway</u> <u>settled</u> in the <u>Americas</u> <u>500</u> years <u>before</u> <u>Columbus</u>. They took <u>160</u> <u>settlers</u> to a colony that lasted <u>3</u> <u>years</u>. A <u>boy</u> named <u>Snorri</u> <u>Karlsefni</u> was <u>born</u> there.

(15 facts)

31   © 1997 Thinking Publications
Listen and Recall

Largest Quilt

The w<u>orld's</u> <u>largest</u> <u>quil</u>t was <u>made</u> by the people of <u>Rollegem</u>, <u>Belgium</u>, in <u>1982</u>. It measures about <u>771</u> <u>square</u> <u>yards</u> and weighs <u>913</u> <u>pounds</u>. <u>Sixteen</u> and <u>eight-tenths</u> <u>miles</u> of <u>thread</u> were used.

(13 facts)

32   © 1997 Thinking Publications
Listen and Recall

© 1997 Thinking Publications. Duplication permitted for educational use only.

Human Spider

On <u>November</u> <u>11</u>, <u>1981</u>, <u>Dan</u> <u>Goodwin</u> <u>climbed</u> the <u>outside</u> of the <u>100</u>-<u>story</u> <u>John</u> <u>Hancock</u> <u>Center</u> in <u>Chicago</u>, <u>Illinois</u>. It took <u>6</u> <u>hours</u> to climb the <u>east side</u> of the <u>1,127</u>-<u>foot</u> building. He was <u>arrested</u> when he finished.

(20 facts)

© 1997 Thinking Publications
Listen and Recall

No Way to Travel

In <u>July</u> of <u>1982</u>, <u>Larry</u> <u>Walters</u> tried to <u>float</u> across the <u>Mojave Desert</u> in <u>California</u>. He <u>attached</u> <u>balloons</u> to a <u>lawn chair</u>. He went up <u>16,000</u> <u>feet</u>. It became so <u>cold</u> that he began to <u>break</u> the balloons. He came down through <u>power lines</u> and caused a <u>blackout</u> in <u>Long Beach</u>, <u>California</u>, that lasted for <u>20</u> <u>minutes</u>.

(20 facts)

© 1997 Thinking Publications
Listen and Recall

© 1997 Thinking Publications. Duplication permitted for educational use only.

Talking Teeth

It was 4 a.m. on Monday, February 12, 1980. George Dillard of Riverhead, New York, heard voices in his head. He called the police. A police officer, David Cheshire, figured out it was George's new dentures. They were picking up a radio station from Connecticut.

(19 facts)

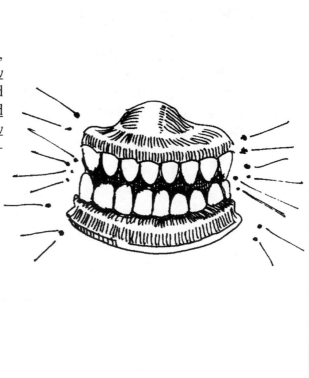

© 1997 Thinking Publications
Listen and Recall

A Brave Woman

Harriet Tubman was born as a slave about 1821. She escaped from Broadas Plantation in Maryland. She was nicknamed Moses because she returned about 19 times to guide others to freedom. More than $40,000 (forty-thousand dollars) in rewards were offered for her capture.

(20 facts)

© 1997 Thinking Publications
Listen and Recall

© 1997 Thinking Publications. Duplication permitted for educational use only.

First Men to the North Pole

<u>Matthew</u> <u>A</u>. <u>Henson</u>, a <u>black</u> <u>explorer</u>, <u>planted</u> the <u>United States</u> <u>flag</u> at the <u>North Pole</u> on <u>April</u> <u>6</u>, <u>1909</u>. He and <u>Rear Admiral</u> <u>Robert</u> <u>E</u>. <u>Perry</u> had <u>tried several times</u> in <u>18</u> <u>years</u> to reach the North Pole. This time they <u>traveled</u> <u>400</u> <u>miles</u>. <u>Perry</u> had <u>lost</u> <u>8</u> of his <u>toes</u> on <u>previous trips</u>.

(27 facts)

© 1997 Thinking Publications
Listen and Recall

37

A Great Scientist

<u>George</u> <u>Washington</u> <u>Carver</u> was a <u>college</u> <u>professor</u> at <u>Tuskegee</u> <u>Institute</u> in <u>Alabama</u>. He began teaching there in <u>1896</u>. He was <u>paid</u> $1,500 (<u>fifteen hundred</u> <u>dollars</u>) <u>per year</u>. He was <u>offered</u> a $50,000-<u>per-year</u> (<u>fifty thousand</u> <u>dollars</u>) job by <u>Thomas Edison</u>, but he turned it down so he could continue his work.

(18 facts)

© 1997 Thinking Publications
Listen and Recall

38

© 1997 Thinking Publications. Duplication permitted for educational use only.

First Circus

The <u>first</u> <u>circus</u> in the <u>United States</u> opened in <u>Philadelphia</u> on <u>April</u> <u>3</u>, <u>1793</u>. It included a <u>clown</u>, a <u>rope walker</u>, and a <u>horse</u> named <u>Cornplanter</u>. <u>John</u> <u>Bill</u> <u>Ricketts</u> <u>owned</u> the circus. <u>Eight</u> <u>hundred</u> <u>people</u> could see <u>each show</u>. <u>George</u> <u>Washington</u> and <u>John</u> <u>Adams</u> <u>saw</u> <u>the performance</u>.

(23 facts)

39 © 1997 Thinking Publications
Listen and Recall

Burial Suit

In <u>China</u>, the <u>Han</u> <u>dynasty</u> was <u>from</u> <u>206</u> <u>B.C.</u> to <u>221</u> <u>A.D</u>. When <u>Prince</u> <u>Liu</u> <u>Sheng</u> <u>died</u>, his <u>body</u> was <u>covered</u> with <u>2,498</u> <u>pieces of jade</u>. They were <u>held together</u> by <u>knots</u> and <u>gold wire</u>.

(19 facts)

40 © 1997 Thinking Publications
Listen and Recall

© 1997 Thinking Publications. Duplication permitted for educational use only.

First Electric Subway

The <u>first</u> e<u>lectric</u> <u>subway</u> was built in <u>Budapest</u>, <u>Hungary</u>. It was <u>opened</u> on <u>May</u> <u>8</u>, <u>1896</u>. It was originally <u>named</u> <u>after</u> <u>Franz</u> <u>Joseph</u>, the <u>Austro-Hungarian</u> <u>emperor</u>. Franz Joseph r<u>ode</u> <u>the</u> subway <u>that</u> <u>day</u>. <u>Seven</u> <u>hundred</u> <u>thousand</u> <u>passengers</u> still use the Budapest subway <u>each</u> <u>workday</u>. It has <u>survived</u> <u>two</u> <u>world</u> <u>war</u>s.

(22 facts)

© 1997 Thinking Publications
Listen and Recall

Tallest and Deepest

The tallest mountain is <u>Mt. Everest</u> in <u>Nepal</u>-<u>Tibet</u>. It is more than <u>29,028</u> f<u>eet</u> <u>above</u> <u>sea level</u>. The deepest part of the ocean is <u>Mariana</u> <u>Trench</u> in the <u>Pacific</u>. It is <u>35,810</u> f<u>eet</u> <u>deep</u>.

(11 facts)

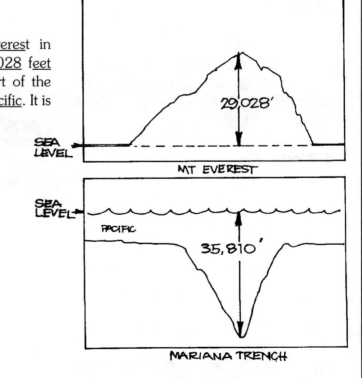

© 1997 Thinking Publications
Listen and Recall

© 1997 Thinking Publications. Duplication permitted for educational use only.

Oldest Underwater Wreck

A <u>ship</u> w<u>ent down</u> off <u>Cape</u> <u>Ulu</u> <u>Burun</u>, <u>Turkey</u>. It sank more than <u>3,400</u> <u>years</u> ago (<u>1400</u> <u>B.C.</u>). <u>Scientists</u> have <u>found</u> <u>pottery</u>, <u>goblets</u>, an <u>elephant tus</u>k, and a <u>hippopotamus tooth</u>. <u>Dr.</u> <u>George</u> <u>F.</u> <u>Bass</u> of <u>Texas</u> <u>A</u> and <u>M</u> <u>University</u> is the <u>chief scientist</u>.

(25 facts)

43   © 1997 Thinking Publications
Listen and Recall

Refused Letters

In <u>1885</u>, <u>Susan</u> <u>B.</u> <u>Anthony</u>, who worked for w<u>omen's rights</u>, <u>visited</u> <u>Germany</u>. She <u>wrote</u> <u>several letters</u>. <u>On the envelopes</u>, she wrote <u>slogans</u> such as "<u>Taxation without representation</u> is <u>tyranny</u>." The <u>German</u> <u>post office</u>, <u>under</u> <u>Otto</u> von <u>Bismarck</u>, <u>refused</u> to send the letters because of the slogans.

(21 facts)

44   © 1997 Thinking Publications
Listen and Recall

© 1997 Thinking Publications. Duplication permitted for educational use only.

Musical Joke

As a joke in early 1961, people at the British Broadcasting Company played 12 minutes of random noises. They pretended it was music. They called it "Mobile for Tape and Percussion" by Piortr Zak. They fooled many people, even music critics.

(21 facts)

45   © 1997 Thinking Publications
Listen and Recall

A Historic Fall

On March 5, 1775, there was a meeting at Old South Meeting House in Boston. It was the fifth anniversary of the Boston Massacre. Samuel Adams, John Hancock, and Joseph Warren were leaders at the meeting. The British planned to arrest the three leaders. A British soldier would signal the arrest by throwing an egg at the men. On the way to the meeting, the soldier fell and broke the egg. No arrests were made that day.

(26 facts)

46   © 1997 Thinking Publications
Listen and Recall

    © 1997 Thinking Publications. Duplication permitted for educational use only.

Collapsed Mountain

Mt. Mazama was 9,900 feet high. It was a volcano. About 7,000 years ago, it "blew." The top of the mountain collapsed, forming a hole 6 miles across and a half mile deep. It is now filled with water. It is Crater Lake in southern Oregon.

(20 facts)

© 1997 Thinking Publications
Listen and Recall

A Musical Message

Prince Nicolaus Esterhazy had a summer castle in a lonely part of Hungary. He kept several musicians working there without their families. In 1772, Franz Joseph Haydn wrote a special symphony to show the prince that they were lonely. As they were playing the music, one musician would finish his part, blow out his candle, and leave. Then another musician left, and another, until only two were left. The prince let them go on vacation the next day.

(27 facts)

© 1997 Thinking Publications
Listen and Recall

© 1997 Thinking Publications. Duplication permitted for educational use only.

A Big Nobel Prize

<u>Dr</u>. <u>Carlo</u> <u>Rubbia</u> was given a <u>Nobel prize</u> in <u>physics</u> on <u>December 10, 1984</u>. He was responsible for having the w<u>orld's largest particle smashing instrument</u> built. It is <u>4 miles</u> in <u>circumference</u>. It is <u>under</u> the <u>border</u> of <u>France</u> and <u>Switzerland</u>.

(17 facts)

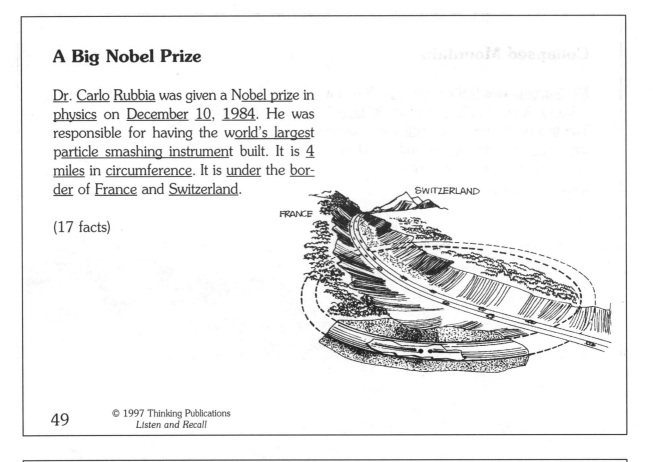

SWITZERLAND

FRANCE

© 1997 Thinking Publications
Listen and Recall

49

Musical Fireworks

A <u>treaty</u> was signed to end the <u>War</u> of <u>Austrian</u> <u>Succession</u>. Preparations for a <u>celebration</u> took <u>6</u> <u>months</u>. A h<u>uge structure</u> was built in <u>London's</u> <u>Green</u> <u>Park</u>. <u>George</u> <u>Frederick</u> <u>Handel</u> <u>composed</u> a piece called "<u>Music</u> <u>for</u> <u>the</u> <u>Royal</u> <u>Fireworks</u>." The musical performance included <u>cannons</u> and <u>fireworks</u>. The celebration was held on <u>April</u> <u>27</u>, <u>1749</u>. As the music reached its <u>climax</u>, the special celebration structure accidentally <u>caught fire</u>. <u>Rockets</u> whizzed by. People had to <u>flee</u>.

(29 facts)

© 1997 Thinking Publications
Listen and Recall

50

© 1997 Thinking Publications. Duplication permitted for educational use only.

Maps

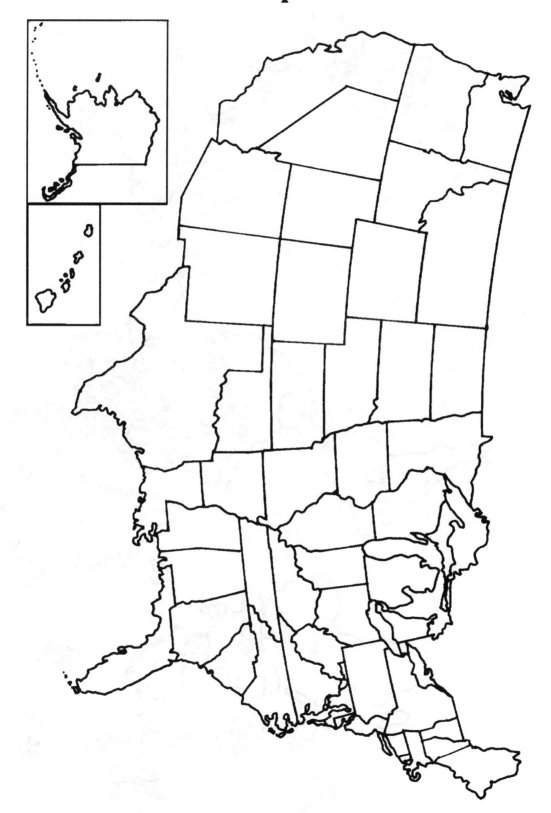

© 1997 Thinking Publications. Duplication permitted for educational use only.

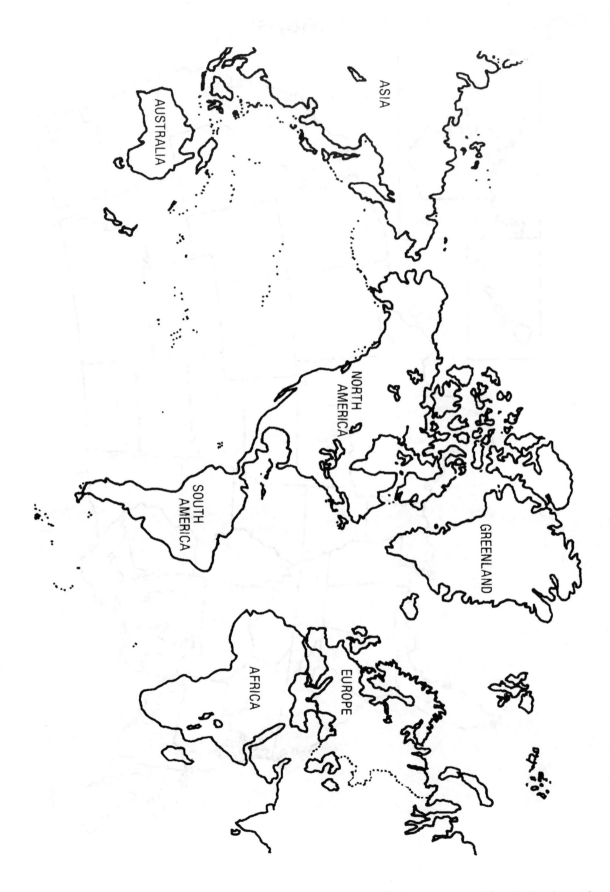

© 1997 Thinking Publications. Duplication permitted for educational use only.

Counting Facts

The examples below demonstrate the fact-counting system suggested for *Listen and Recall*. It will become clear from the examples, and in working with listeners, that the counting system is only a guide and that the adult providing intervention will need to use professional judgment when counting facts recalled. As mentioned on pages 47–49 in Section II, the listener's progress can be monitored by counting recalled facts such as names, numbers, and dates.

Example 1: Ice Age Drawings

In this example, considerable help is given during presentation of the facts, as indicated by the comments in parentheses. The adult providing intervention shows listeners the illustration and makes a brief statement about a young girl making an important discovery.

In 1879 (pause to discuss strategies for remembering this date), a 9-year-old girl (pause again to discuss how *9* can be remembered) was exploring Altamira Cave (pause to discuss techniques for recall of this name) in Spain (pause). She discovered drawings on the wall. The girl, Maria, (pause) had found drawings that were 16,000 years old. *(Ice Age is omitted because it is felt that the listeners have enough to remember, based on their facial expressions.)*

Facts to be Recalled	Potential Credit	Rationale
1879	1 fact	One fact is counted for the year since it must be remembered as a unit.
9-year-old girl	2 facts	The number *9* is counted as one fact and *year,* the unit of measurement, is also counted as a fact. *Girl* is not counted because the gender of the child becomes apparent later when the name is revealed.
exploring	1 fact	One fact is counted for the main activity described on the *Stimulus Card.*
Altamira Cave	2 facts	Credit is given for each part of an unfamiliar location.
Spain	1 fact	Credit is given for a name.
drawings	1 fact	Credit is given for what is discovered in the cave.
Maria	1 fact	Credit is given for a name.
16,000 years	2 facts	The number *16,000* is counted as one fact and the unit of measurement is counted as another one.
Total:	11 facts	

Questions Asked by Adult	Listener Response	Credit and Explanation
When did this happen?	1979	No credit is given.
What was her name?	Maria	1 fact
How old was she?	9 years old	2 facts
Where did she do this?	Alta something	No credit is given, but association techniques can be discussed and encouragement given for the partial answer.
What was she doing in the cave?	exploring	1 fact
What did she find in the cave?	drawings	1 fact
Do you remember the country?	Spain	1 fact
How old were the drawings?	14,000 years old	1 fact (for *years*)
Total:	7 facts	

Score: Seven out of eleven facts were recalled, with some help provided during presentation of the information. The listener applied association and visualization techniques with the active assistance of the adult providing intervention. This score is recorded as "7/11 w/help."

Example 2: Tallest and Deepest

In this example, some help is given during presentation of the facts, as indicated in parentheses. The adult providing intervention shows listeners the illustration and briefly discusses what it represents: that the ocean bottom can be very deep and the mountains extremely high.

The tallest mountain is Mt. Everest (pause and verbally encourage the listener to associate *the tallest* with the name *Everest*) in Nepal-Tibet (pause). It is more than 29,000 feet above sea level. (The exact number, 29,028, can be used instead with more capable listeners.) The deepest part of the ocean is Mariana Trench (verbally encourage the listener to make another specific association, such as looking down, which would be kinesthetic imagery, to see "Mary Ann in a trench") in the Pacific. It is more than 35,800 feet deep. (The full number can be used, as mentioned before, or *nearly 36,000* would be more simple to recall.)

Facts to be Recalled	Potential Credit	Rationale
Mt. Everest	1 fact	This fact is a well-known place and is thought of as one concept by most people.
Nepal-Tibet	2 facts	There are two names given here.
29,000 feet above sea level	3 facts	One fact is counted for *29,000*; one fact is counted for *feet*, which is the unit of measurement; *sea level* is counted as the third fact.
Mariana Trench	2 facts	Each part of a longer name receives a credit.
Pacific	1 fact	Credit is given for a name.
35,800 feet deep	2 facts	One fact is counted for the number and one for the unit of measurement *feet. Deep* is not counted because the adult providing intervention asks "How deep is it?"
Total:	11 facts	

Questions Asked by Adult	Listener Response	Credit and Explanation
What's the name of the tallest mountain?	Mt. Everest	1 fact
Where is it?	I don't remember.	No credit
How tall is it?	2,900 feet high	1 fact is credited for *feet. 2,900* was substituted for *29,000* so that fact is not counted as correct.
What is the name of the deepest part of the ocean?	Mary Ann Ditch	1 fact; credit is given for *Mary Ann* because it is so close to *Mariana*; however, none is given for *Ditch.* The substitutions of *Ditch* for *Trench* and *Mary Ann* for *Mariana* are discussed with the listener to improve precision of retention and retrieval strategies.
Where is it?	Pacific	1 fact
How deep is it?	35,000 feet	1 fact for *feet*, the unit of measurement; the adult providing intervention might also credit the number as a correctly recalled fact if he or she determines it is acceptably deviant from the actual number presented to the listener.
Total:	5 facts	

Score: Five out of eleven facts were recalled, with assistance given to aid retention. This is recorded as "8/11 w/help."

References

Adams, W., and Sheslow, D. (1990). *Wide range assessment of memory and learning.* Wilmington, DE: Wide Range.

Alley, G., and Deshler, D. (1979). *Teaching the learning disabled adolescent: Strategies and methods.* Denver, CO: Love Publishing.

Annett, J. (1995). Imagery and motor processes: Editorial overview. *British Journal of Psychology, 86,* 161–167.

Ashcraft, M.H. (1990). Strategic processing in children's mental arithmetic: A review and proposal. In D.F. Bjorklund (Ed.), *Children's strategies: Contemporary views of cognitive development* (pp. 185–211). Hillsdale, NJ: Erlbaum.

Baker, H., and Leland, B. (1967). *Detroit tests of learning aptitude.* Indianapolis, IN: Merrill.

Bjorklund, D.F., and Harnishfeyer, K.K. (1990). Children's strategies: Their definition and origins. In D.F. Bjorklund (Ed.), *Children's strategies: Contemporary views of cognitive development* (pp. 309–323). Hillsdale, NJ: Erlbaum.

Bjorklund, D.F., Muir-Broaddus, J.E., and Schneider, W. (1990). The role of knowledge in the development of strategies. In D.F. Bjorklund (Ed.), *Children's strategies: Contemporary views of cognitive development* (pp. 93–128). Hillsdale, NJ: Erlbaum.

Bower, G. (1970). Imagery as a relational organizer in associative learning. *Journal of Verbal Learning and Verbal Behavior, 9,* 529–533.

Bower, G., and Winzenz, D. (1970). Comparison of associative learning strategies. *Psychonomic Science, 20,* 119–120.

Bryan, T., and Bryan, J. (1978). *Understanding learning disabilities* (2nd ed.). Sherman Oaks, CA: Alfred Publishing.

Carlisle, J.F. (1990). Diagnostic assessment of listening and reading comprehension. In H.L. Swanson and B. Keogh (Eds.), *Learning disabilities: Theoretical and research issues* (pp. 277–298). Hillsdale, NJ: Erlbaum.

Carpenter, P., Just, M., and Shell, P. (1990). What one intelligence test measures: A theoretical account of the processing in the Raven progressive matrices test. *Psychological Review, 97,* 404–431.

Ceci, S., Ringstrom, M., and Lea, S. (1981). Do language-learning disabled children (L/LDs) have impaired memories? In search of underlying processes. *Journal of Learning Disabilities, 14,* 159–173.

Cowan, N. (1996). Short-term memory, working memory, and language processing. *Topics in Language Disorders, 17*(1), 1–18.

Craik, F., and Tulving, E. (1975). Depth of processing and the retention of words in episodic memory. *Journal of Experimental Psychology, 1,* 268–294.

Crosson, B., and Buenning, W. (1984). An individualized memory retraining program after closed-head injury: A single-case study. *Journal of Clinical Neuropsychology, 6,* 287–301.

Dansereau, D.F. (1985). Learning strategy research. In J.W. Segal, S.F. Chapman, and R. Galsser (Eds.), *Thinking and learning skills* (Vol. 1). Hillsdale, NJ: Erlbaum.

Deshler, D.D., Schumaker, J.B., and Lenz, B.K. (1984a). Academic and cognitive interventions for L.D. adolescents: Part 1. *Journal of Learning Disabilities, 17,* 108–117.

Deshler, D.D., Schumaker, J.B., and Lenz, B.K. (1984b). Academic and cognitive interventions for L.D. adolescents: Part II. *Journal of Learning Disabilities, 17,* 170–179.

Donaldson, W., and Boss, M. (1980). Relational information and memory for problem solutions. *Journal of Verbal Learning and Verbal Behavior, 19,* 26–35.

Eysenck, M. (1977). *Human memory theory, research and individual differences.* New York: Pergamon Press.

Folds, T.H., Footo, M.M., Guttentag, R.E., and Ornstein, P. (1990). When children mean to remember: Issues of context specificity, strategy effectiveness, and intentionality in the development of memory. In D.F. Bjorklund (Ed.), *Children's strategies: Contemporary views of cognitive development* (pp. 69–92). Hillsdale, NJ: Erlbaum.

Godfrey, H., and Knight, R. (1988). Memory training and behavioral rehabilitation of a severely head-injured adult. *Archives of Physical Medicine Rehabilitation, 69,* 458–460.

Hammill, D. (1985). *Detroit tests of learning aptitude* (2nd ed.). Austin, TX: Pro-Ed.

Hammill, D. (1991). *Detroit tests of learning aptitude* (3rd ed.). Austin TX: Pro-Ed.

Hammill, D.D., Brown, V.L., Larsen, S.C., and Wiederholt, J.L. (1987). *Test of adolescent and adult language* (3rd ed.). Austin, TX: Pro-Ed.

Hammill, D., and Bryant, B.R. (1991). *Detroit tests of learning aptitude–adult.* Austin, TX: Pro-Ed.

Harrell, M., Parenté, R., Bellingrath, E.G., and Lisicia, K.A. (1992). *Cognitive rehabilitation of memory: A practical guide.* Gaithersburg, MD: Aspen.

Higbee, K.L. (1988). *Your memory* (2nd ed.). Englewood Cliffs, NJ: Prentice-Hall.

Jacoby, L. (1978). On interpreting the effects of repetition: Solving a problem vs. remembering a solution. *Journal of Verbal Learning and Verbal Behavior, 17,* 649–667.

Kirchner, D.M., and Klatzky, R.L. (1985). Verbal rehearsal and memory in language-disordered children. *Journal of Speech and Hearing Research, 28,* 556–565.

Lahey, M., and Bloom, L. (1994). Variability and language learning disabilities. In G. Wallach and K. Butler (Eds.), *Language learning disabilities in school-age children and adolescents* (pp. 354–372). New York: Macmillan.

Lorsbach, T.C., and Gray, J.W. (1985). The development of encoding processes in L.D. children. *Journal of Learning Disabilities, 18*(4), 222–227.

McDaniel, M.A., and Pressley, M. (1987). *Imagery and related mnemonic processes: Theories, individual differences and applications.* New York: Springer-Verlag.

McFarland, C., Jr., Frey, T., and Rhodes, D. (1980). Retrieval of internally vs. externally generated words in episodic visual presentation. *Journal of Verbal Learning and Verbal Behavior, 19,* 210–225.

Montgomery, J. (1996). Sentence comprehension and working memory in children with specific language impairment. *Topics in Language Disorders, 17*(1), 19–32.

Moscovitch, M., and Craik, F. (1976). Depth of processing, retrieval cues, and uniqueness of encoding as factors in recall. *Journal of Verbal Learning and Verbal Behavior, 15,* 447–458.

Naito, M., and Komatsu, S. (1993). Processes involved in childhood development of implicit memory. In P. Graf and M.E.J. Masson (Eds.), *Implicit memory: New directions in cognition, development and neuropsychology* (pp. 231–260). Hillsdale, NJ: Erlbaum.

Neisser, U. (1976). *Cognition and reality: Principles and implications of cognitive psychology.* San Francisco, CA: Freeman.

Neisser, U., and Winograd, E. (1988). *Remembering reconsidered: Ecological and traditional approaches to the study of memory.* New York: Cambridge University Press.

Parenté, R., and Herrmann, D. (1996). Retraining memory strategies. *Topics in Language Disorders, 17*(1), 45–57.

Pressley, M., Forest-Pressley, D.L., Elliott-Faust, D., and Miller, G. (1985). Children's use of cognitive strategies, how to teach strategies, and what to do if they can't be taught. In M. Pressley and C.J. Brainerd (Eds.), *Cognitive learning and memory in children* (pp. 1–47). New York: Springer-Verlag.

Pressley, M., Symons, S., Snyder, B.L., and Cariglia-Bull, T. (1989). Strategy instruction research comes of age. *Learning Disabilities Quarterly, 12*(1), 16–31.

Rampp, D. (1980). *Auditory processing and learning disabilities.* Lincoln, NE: Cliff Notes.

Reynolds, C.R., and Bigler, E.D. (1994). *Test of memory and learning.* Austin, TX: Pro-Ed.

Richardson, J.T.E. (1992). Imagery mnemonics and memory remediation. *Neurology, 42,* 283–286.

Schmidt, J.P., and Tombaugh, T.N. (1995). *The learning and memory battery.* North Tonawanda, NY: MHS.

Schneider, W., and Pressley, M. (1989). *Memory development between 2 and 20.* New York: Springer-Verlag.

Scruggs, T.E., and Mastropieri, M.A. (1989). Mnemonic instruction of LD students: A field based evaluation. *Learning Disabilities Quarterly, 12*(2),119–132.

Semel, E., and Wiig, E. (1980). *Clinical evaluation of language functions.* Columbus, OH: Merrill.

Semel, E., Wiig, E.H., and Secord, W.A. (1995). *Clinical evaluation of language fundamentals* (3rd ed.). San Antonio, TX: Psychological Corporation.

Semel, E., Wiig, E.H., Secord, W.A., and Sabers, D. (1987). *Clinical evaluation of language fundamentals–revised.* San Antonio, TX: Psychological Corporation.

Slamecka, J., and Graf, P. (1978). The generation effect. *Journal of Experimental Psychology, 4*, 592–604.

Swanson, H.L. (1990). Instruction derived from the strategy deficit model: Overview of principles and procedures. In T.E. Scruggs and B.Y.L. Wong (Eds.), *Intervention research in learning disabilities* (pp. 34–65). New York: Springer-Verlag.

Walker, S.C., and Poteet, J. (1989). Influencing memory performance in learning disabled students through semantic processing. *Learning Disabilities Research, 5*(1), 25–32.

Walsh, D., and Jenkins, J. (1973). Effects of orienting tasks on free recall in incidental learning: "Difficulty," "effort," and "process" explanations. *Journal of Verbal Learning and Verbal Behavior, 12*, 481–488.

Wechsler, D. (1981). *Wechsler adult intelligence scale* (Rev. ed.). San Antonio, TX: Psychological Corporation.

Wechsler, D. (1974). *Wechsler intelligence scale for children* (Rev. ed.). San Antonio, TX: Psychological Corporation.

Wechsler, D. (1991). *Wechsler intelligence scale for children* (3rd ed.) San Antonio, TX: Psychological Corporation.

Wiig, E., and Semel, E. (1980). *Language assessment and intervention for the learning disabled.* Columbus, OH: Merrill.

Wood, M. (1982). *Language disorders in school-age children.* Englewood Cliffs, NJ: Prentice-Hall.

Woodcock, R.W., and Johnson, M. Bonner. (1989, 1990). *Woodcock-Johnson psycho-educational battery–revised: Tests of cognitive ability.* Chicago: Riverside.